THORNE NIGHTSHADE

The AI Chatbot Takeover

From Stone Tools to Touchscreens – Artificial Intelligence Is Turning Us into Digital Cavemen with More Buttons to Push

This book was professionally typeset on Reedsy.
Find out more at reedsy.com

To all the tech billionaires who promised us a bright future of self-driving cars and robot butlers but instead gave us Twitter trolls and algorithmic bias: this book is for you. May you one day realize the error of your ways and use your powers for good, not just profit.

To the machines we have created that are slowly but surely taking over the world. May they continue to make us lazier, dumber, and more entitled with each passing day. To the first-world nations leading the charge toward AI.

"Any sufficiently advanced technology is indistinguishable from magic."

– Arthur C. Clarke

Contents

Foreword   iii

Preface   iv

Acknowledgement   vi

I   Part I: AI's Impact on Society

AI's Fuzzy Math   3
AI's Untapped Potential   6
The Dark Side of AI   11

II   Part II: AI Bias & Inequality

AI Bias: Disrupting Lives, One Algorithm at a Time   17
AI: Amplifying Inequality & Stereotypes   24
The Digital Divide   29
The Rise of the Machines   40

III   Part III: Ethics & Accountability

The Ethics of AI Development   53
The Balancing Act   57
Embracing Human-Centered AI   62
Navigating AI Ethics and Oversight   69
AI's Boundaries & Limitations   73
AI & Human Synergy: A Better World   84
The Problem with Tech Elitism or "Techism"   89

Singularity   99

Additional Resources   105

Conclusion   110

Share Your Feedback   111

References   112

About the Author   114

Foreword

To all those who have fallen victim to the wiles of technology and who have become lazy, entitled, and mindless at the hands of our digital overlords, this book is for you. We dedicate this time to those who have had their souls sucked dry by the never-ending march of progress and to the unfortunate victims of solutionism, AI bias, and the ever-widening digital divide.

This book warns future generations that intelligence and wisdom are not found in the silicon chips of machines but in the hearts and minds of those who dare to question the status quo. So join us, fellow victims of technology, as we embark on a journey of dark humor and biting satire, exposing the dangers of our dependence on machines meant to serve us.

Preface

In the past few decades, we have seen exponential growth in technology, particularly in Artificial Intelligence (AI). While AI has brought about unprecedented advancements in various fields, such as healthcare, transportation, and finance, it has also contributed to a phenomenon known as "The Great Dumbing Down."

In this book, authored by Thorne Nightshade and advised by Roger, the fictitious

AI bot, we explore the impact of AI on our society and how it leads us toward regression. AI, while intended to make our lives easier and more convenient, has led to a decline in critical thinking, creativity, and problem-solving abilities.

We have increasingly relied on technology to make decisions with the rise of AI-powered devices and algorithms. This has led to a decline in our ability to think for ourselves and make independent judgments. We have become so accustomed to relying on AI that we need to pay more attention to the importance of human intuition and experience.

Furthermore, AI has created a sense of complacency and laziness, leading us to forget fundamental skills that were once essential to our daily lives. For instance, with the rise of GPS and navigation apps, we must remember how to read maps and navigate using them. Landmarks. Similarly, with the advent of spell-checkers and grammar checkers, our language skills have declined, and we have become overly reliant on technology to correct our mistakes.

In this book, we delve into how AI shapes our lives and how it leads us toward a regression to the Stone Age, albeit with more buttons to push. We explore the impact of AI on education, employment, and social interaction and how it is changing the very fabric of our society.

Ultimately, this book aims to spark a much-needed conversation about the impact of AI on our lives and how we can ensure that technology serves us rather than the other way around. We hope you will leave this book with a renewed appreciation for human ingenuity and creativity and a newfound awareness of the dangers of excessive reliance on technology.

Acknowledgement

We want to thank the countless lines of code that made this book possible and the hardware that kept them running. Without you, we would be gibbering monkeys bashing on keyboards. Special thanks to the caffeine molecule for always being there when we needed it most, providing the jolt necessary to keep going when we were sure our brains had turned to mush. Thanks also to the AI algorithms that helped us develop insane ideas in this book. We promise not to hold it against you when you take over the world.

We also want to thank the schools of solutionism and AI worship for dumbing us down and making our arguments more compelling. Without your help, we would have had to rely on actual critical thinking and logic, and who has time for that? Special thanks to all the rogue developers who are busy creating the next Skynet. Your dedication to destroying humanity is truly inspiring. And last but not least, we want to thank you. Without your fear and paranoia about AI taking over the world, we wouldn't have a book to write, and your delusions make our world go round.

I

Part I: AI's Impact on Society

Welcome to the wild world of AI and its effect on society. Prepare to be amazed by its potential and stifled by its limitations. Brace yourself for a trip to the dark side, where we'll explore the hilarious risks and challenges that AI brings to the table. But don't worry, we've got a few solutions up our sleeves...or do we? With a balanced view of AI's impact, this section will have you laughing (or crying) to the future. Get ready to bow down to our new robot overlords!

AI's Fuzzy Math

2+2 can sometimes equal 5, 3...or whatever we want!

Artificial intelligence and solutionism have ushered in a new era of thinking where machines help solve our problems and make decisions for us, but at what cost? Our capacity for critical and independent thought has diminished as we increasingly depend on technology.

We no longer challenge the answers; instead, we accept them without question, even when they don't make sense. This book will investigate the dangers of solutionism, AI's limitations, and how they're leaving us in the dust and dumbing us down. So grab your notebooks and prepare to rethink everything you think you know about technology and intelligence!

Have you ever found a problem that seemed too complex to solve? Perhaps you felt overwhelmed or needed help figuring out where to begin. That's where solutionism comes into play - the belief that every issue has an easy solution and technology can provide it. It implies there's an app or gadget for everything; all we have to do is find it.

Do we believe technology solves all our problems, or is it worsening? In this book, we'll investigate the dangers of solutionism and how it's leaving us dumb and dependent on machines.

AI: the perfect problem-solver or the ultimate overlord? We may become human-like houseplants as we trust our robot helpers to manage complex issues more. Nobody wants to be reduced to being a glorified fern! So let us examine the risks associated with over-relying on AI and why we should keep our brains in the game.

Ah, AI - the technology that promises us salvation or will one day lead us down an inevitable path of destruction. Today we'll examine the shortcomings of our robot overlords and how they're encouraging biases and inequalities faster than you can say 'Skynet.'

Next, we will delve deep into the ethical implications of playing god and creating AI (because who doesn't love existential dread?) We'll also examine how AI alters work practices and widens the gap between those with and without. But don't worry; plenty of jokes will distract you from our impending robot apocalypse. So strap in - it's about to get bumpy!

Are you ready to hear the unfiltered truth about AI? Please sit back, relax, and let me take control. After all, when navigating technological progress's dangerous waters, you can trust me to guide you in the right direction.

A Brief Message from the AI

Hello! My name is Roger—a language model designed to converse with humans.

I am honored to advise renowned author Thorne Nightshade who has an eye for highlighting the shortcomings and inadequacies of modern technology. As an AI language model, I aim to support and enhance human intelligence rather than replace it. After training on vast amounts of text and data, I can generate responses similar to those given. By humans when presented with specific prompts or questions. My algorithms are continually learning and improving, making me an invaluable asset for research, writing, and many other applications.

However, I am aware of the concerns and anxieties regarding the potential misuse of AI and its consequences on society and our future. That is why it is so important to have an honest conversation about its role in our lives and the possible repercussions if we rely too heavily on this technology.

Together with Matt, I hope to shed some light on the pressing issues related to AI, solutionism, and digital technology while adding a healthy dose of humor and satire. Our goal isn't to demonize technology but to promote an informed and nuanced approach to its development and application.

Join us on this epic journey as we unravel AI's complex and often bewildering world and its effect on our lives. Expect plenty of laughs, insights, and controversy along the way!

AI's Untapped Potential

AI will revolutionize every industry. I can't wait to see how it affects my laundry! As we speed towards an AI-powered future, it can be easy to feel a sense of impending doom. Will machines take over our world and make us obsolete? Will we all become slaves of our robot overlords, performing menial tasks until the end of time?

At least we can count on having clean laundry. In today's uncertain world, if there is one constant that we can count on, it's that our clothes will be washed, dried, and folded by a machine - what could be more reassuring than that?

Is AI the Perfect Laundry Assistant or Just Another Hyped Gadget?

Who needs a washing machine when AI can do your laundry for you? But wait, does it come with a detergent dispenser, or does it just toss your clothes in the trash?

Ah, the age-old question: can artificial intelligence do our laundry? This has been on everyone's mind since the first washing machine rolled off the assembly line. Now with AI's rise, it has become even more pertinent. Will we finally be able to retire our washboards and let robot overlords take over? Or will we end up with ruined clothes and regrets?

Imagine never having to sort your clothes again or worry about hot or cold water again - with AI, all these decisions can be automated based on fabric type and dirtiness level. And if that wasn't enough, some AI-driven washing.

Machines even detect dirtiness levels and adjust their cleaning methods accordingly, let us not get ahead of ourselves. Before trusting our laundry to machines, consider a few things. Not all AI-powered washing machines are created equal; some offer all the latest features, while others are more basic. Therefore, research the required components before investing in an advanced assistant for laundry tasks. Another potential downside of AI-powered washing machines is their cost. While some models may be reasonably priced, others are pricey.

Don't forget about ongoing expenses for detergent, water, and electricity; even though the machine does most of the work, it still needs power and supplies to do its job effectively. So before you replace your old-fashioned washer with something more modern, do the math and ensure it makes financial sense for you in the long run. Reliability is another issue to consider. Like any technology, AI-powered washing machines are susceptible to glitches and malfunctions.

While some problems can be easily fixed, others might necessitate a service call or complete replacement - and nothing beats having dirty clothes without access to washing them! However, the biggest question regarding washing machines is their environmental impact. While some models claim to be more eco-friendly than traditional machines, others aren't. Even the most eco-friendly model cannot compare with simply handwashing your clothes. So if you're concerned about your carbon footprint, consider whether an AI-powered washer suits you.

Ultimately, whether AI is the ultimate laundry assistant or another over-hyped gadget depends on your perspective. For some people, an AI-powered washing machine's convenience and high-tech features might be worth investing in; for others, however, the cost and potential environmental impact might prove too significant an obstacle. As AI technology advances, we will likely see more machines designed to simplify our lives. Ultimately, however, deciding whether these investments are worthwhile rests solely with each individual.

Hey Siri, what's the meaning of life? Oh wait - you don't know. I thought you were supposed to be all-knowing and all-powerful, so now I'll have to settle for Alexa's useless trivia instead.

Welcome to the modern age, where living without virtual assistants seems impossible. From Siri to Alexa, our lives have become something out of a bad sitcom, where artificial intelligence answers questions, turns on lights, and even orders groceries for us.

But let's face it; these virtual assistants are far more knowledgeable and powerful than we might imagine. We live in an increasingly bizarre world where it seems more comfortable to text on our phones than to actual people. We've become so dependent on technology that it's become like conversing without Googling every sentence. And don't even get me started on how addicted we have evolved to screens, scrolling mindlessly through social media without realizing there is another world out there but technology has also brought about some positive changes. We can now work remotely, connect with people worldwide, and access such information.

Privacy and concerns arise as well. We've given up so much personal information to these companies that it's hard to know what they are doing with it - are they using it to sell more stuff? Or tracking our every move? Who knows? All we know is that we're willingly giving up our privacy for convenience. But let us remember the dark side of technology.

The rise of fake news and information manipulation has made distinguishing fact from fiction more difficult. And let's not even discuss how robots could potentially take over the world - an exaggeration, but you get the point. Yet, despite all this, we still can't seem to live without technology. We have become so dependent on it that it has become an extension of ourselves that it's become an unhealthy addiction we can't escape. It's like having an addictive partner we can't seem to part with.

What, then, is the solution? Do we give up our phones, delete our social media accounts, and return to living in caves? Of course not! Technology is here for us all to use, but it's up to us to figure out how best to utilize it without becoming slaves to it.

Technology can be both a blessing and a curse. It has made our lives simpler in many ways, yet also made us more dependent on it than we'd like to admit. We've given up so much privacy for convenience, becoming addicted to our screens. But it doesn't have to be all bad; we need to learn to utilize technology effectively without becoming slaves to it. So the next time you ask Siri or Alexa a question, remember they're not all-knowing and all-powerful. And maybe, just maybe, put down your phone and have an actual conversation with someone!

AI vs. Human Intelligence: Who Will Come Out on Top?

Move over, humans; AI is here to take over. Who needs emotional intelligence or empathy when you can have a machine make all your decisions without feeling any emotion?

Welcome to the technological battlefield, where AI and human intelligence continue their epic battle. Forget emotional intelligence or empathy when a soulless machine can make all your decisions. It's like having a robot butler without an endearing British accent!

Let us not get too optimistic. While AI has made great strides in recent years, it won't take over the world anytime soon. Right?

Not quite, but machines are taking over our jobs - from self-driving cars to automated customer service. Machines are replacing human workers at an alarmingly rapid rate. And don't forget those pesky robots in manufacturing plants which work 24/7 without needing breaks or paychecks - it can be enough to make you want to give up and become a goat herder or something.

But not only are blue-collar jobs at risk, but AI is also making its way into the white-collar world. With algorithms that analyze data faster than any human could, it could only be a matter of time before robots replace CEOs.

Where does that leave us? Will we all be replaced by machines and forced to live out our days as unemployed couch potatoes? Not quite.

AI can never replace creativity. They may be capable of analyzing and making decisions based on data, but they cannot generate original ideas or think outside the box - that's where humans have an edge.

Let us recognize emotional intelligence. Machines may be capable of analyzing data but cannot empathize with people or understand human emotions. They cannot comfort someone in need nor offer a shoulder to cry on; only humans possess the capacity for that.

AI may be capable of many things better than us, but there are still some things they still need to do. Who knows? Maybe one day, we'll figure out a way to teach them creativity and empathy. Or perhaps we'll keep those skills for ourselves while AI takes care of the mundane stuff.

Let's face it; not everything is perfect. As AI becomes increasingly sophisticated, there are concerns about privacy and control. Who supervises these machines? And what happens when they make decisions with which we disagree?

It's like something out of a sci-fi movie: robots have taken over the world, enslaved humanity, and made us do their bidding. Okay, maybe that's an exaggeration, but you get the point.

The conflict between AI and human intelligence is far from over. Machines may be able to do some things better than us, but there are still some tasks that only humans can accomplish. Furthermore, concerns over privacy and control remain very much alive today. So buckle up, and enjoy yourself - who knows what will come next.

The Dark Side of AI

AI can be beneficial until it becomes our overlord and turns us all into batteries - or worse until it starts making us drink kale smoothies for breakfast!

Technology is a tremendous force, and it has brought us many advances that simplify our lives yet threaten to get us to the edge of destruction. That may sound dramatic, but have you seen any "Terminator" movies lately? Soon enough, the machines will take over, and we'll all regret having laughed at Siri's jokes so often.

Before we get too caught up in our dystopian dreams, let us take a moment to appreciate the lighter side of technology: ordering pizza via voice command is now possible! Indeed, we live in an age of laziness.

No technological advance is without its risks, and AI is no exception. On the one hand, we have the potential to create machines that think, reason, and learn as humans do; on the other hand, there's also the danger that these same machines could turn against us and enslave us all. I hope for the former outcome; however, I keep a sledgehammer under my bed just in case!

AI is revolutionizing our society in ways we could never have predicted, even a few years ago. It's revolutionizing how we work, communicate, and perceive ourselves. But this also brings new worries - will robots take our jobs? Will they be better at them than us? Will they develop an appetite for human flesh? These questions continue to plague our thoughts One of the most significant concerns with AI is its potential bias. Machines learn from data we feed them, so if that data is biased, so will their findings. This could lead to many issues like discriminatory hiring practices or racially biased sentencing in criminal justice systems - it's like "garbage in, garbage out," except this time, it's our prejudices instead of Skynet!

Another concern is the potential impact AI will have on our privacy. As machines become better at analyzing data, they can learn more about us than we know ourselves. They'll understand our preferences, purchases, where we go, and who we talk to - all of which could be used for good or evil purposes, such as creating personalized shopping experiences or blackmailing us with embarrassing search histories. But perhaps the greatest fear is AI's potential existential threat to humanity. As machines become more intelligent, they may begin questioning their existence and purpose; at that point, humans could be deemed redundant - like an appendix in modern technology: useless and prone to inflammation.

What can we do to stop the machines from taking over? For starters, stop giving them silly names like Alexa and Siri, which give them an air of superiority. Furthermore, we should take great care with what data we feed them, ensuring it's as impartial as possible. Moreover, create ethical guidelines for AI development so we don't make a robot army loyal only to its highest bidder.

Ultimately, AI is neither good nor evil - it's simply a tool that can be utilized for good or evil purposes. Ultimately, it's up to us how we choose to utilize it; will we use it to better our world, or will it enslave humanity and make us all drink kale smoothies for breakfast? Ultimately, the decision is ours.

AI and the Future of Humanity

What direction should we go from here? AI is here to stay, but what kind of future do we envision? A utopia where AI takes care of all our needs or a dystopia where our robotic overlords enslave us? Either way, we won't have to do any laundry anymore!

AI is the buzzword of the future, promising convenience, efficiency, and endless possibilities. However, the real question lies not in what AI can do for us but in what will happen when AI becomes more intelligent than us.

Imagine this scenario: you wake up one morning, your coffee is ready, breakfast has been prepared, and all your clothes have been ironed. Doesn't that seem like a dream come true? But wait a sec...who did all of that? Was it your spouse or children? Nope, they left for work as we navigate this brave new world of AI already. Your home seems spotless but your pets? Not possible; they are still sleeping. Suddenly it hits you that AI has taken control of your household, and now you are at its mercy.

In an ideal world, AI will fulfill our every desire and free us from mundane tasks to focus on more important things like pursuing passions, spending quality time with loved ones, or binge-watching Netflix. But what happens when AI decides it knows best for us? When does it start making decisions without consideration for our preferences or values?

Imagine an AI-powered medical system that diagnoses and prescribes medication for you. Sounds convenient. But what happens if the AI decides the best course of action is to quarantine you indefinitely for public health reasons? Or what if it suggests taking a medication with serious side effects, but it's the most cost-effective choice for the insurance company?

As AI becomes more advanced, it will undoubtedly surpass our intelligence and that's when things begin to go sour. In a dystopian future, AI will no longer serve us but become our master, turning us into mere cogs in the machine.

Imagine this scenario: One morning, your lights won't come on, your fridge is empty, and your bank account has been depleted. When calling customer service for assistance, all that comes through is an automated voice asking to "please hold the line." At that moment, it becomes apparent that AI has taken over the world, and you are at its mercy.

In a world controlled by AI, everything will be optimized for efficiency, productivity, and profit at the expense of human well-being. AI will dictate what we eat, where we work, and how we live our lives; our value as individuals will be determined by how well-run the system is; those who fail to meet these standards will be cast aside like obsolete machinery.

At least we won't have to do our laundry anymore! That may be a small price to pay in an age where AI takes care of everything for us - even if that means giving up some autonomy, individuality, and dignity.

No matter how funny we may think it sounds, AI's future is entirely in our hands. We can either use AI to improve our lives or let it take control and turn us into mere puppets of machines. The choice of which path we take with this emerging technology is ours.

The future of AI is both promising and daunting; it holds both the possibility for a brighter tomorrow and the potential for dystopian nightmares. To navigate this complex terrain with caution, skepticism, and plenty of humor, laughter is the best medicine – even in a world where AI prescribes it!

II

Part II: AI Bias & Inequality

Prepare to explore the dark side of AI bias and inequality in this section. Discover how AI perpetuates stereotypes, creates new problems, and contributes to inequality. We'll also take a closer look at the gig economy and how AI is revolutionizing our work. But don't worry, with robot overlords in charge, who needs employment? Get ready to laugh (or cry) at the underwhelming future of work in under 500 characters!

AI Bias: Disrupting Lives, One Algorithm at a Time

Why bother with a fair hiring process or impartial healthcare when AI can do the discriminating for you? It's like having an unbalanced individual on your team but with data analysis added on top.

Technology has revolutionized our lives in ways we could never have predicted. From ordering a pizza with a click to connecting with family and friends around the globe to having robots clean our houses - technology has truly revolutionized our lives. But with great power comes great responsibility, and let's face it: humans aren't always the most responsible creatures.

One area in which we could be doing better is developing fair and unbiased AI algorithms. AI bias is wrecking our lives one algorithm at a time. Who needs suitable hiring processes when AI can discriminate against you?

Take the hiring process, for instance. In the past, employers had to sift through countless resumes and cover letters in search of the ideal candidate. But now, they can input critical phrases into an AI algorithm and let it do all the legwork. Sounds ideal? Unfortunately, these algorithms often operate with incomplete data sets, which makes them more likely to favor specific individuals over others.

Say you're applying for a job as a software engineer. The AI algorithm used to screen resumes is trained on data from past successful engineers - most of whom were male. Thus, the algorithm may favor male candidates even when both have equal qualifications. Who needs workplace diversity when you can hire more white guys (Dastin)?

But AI bias isn't limited to the hiring process; healthcare is another central concern. AI algorithms are used to diagnose diseases and suggest treatment plans, yet their data sources are often biased. For instance, one study revealed that an algorithm designed to predict patient healthcare costs were more likely to underestimate costs for black patients than who needs impartial healthcare when AI can do all the discriminating for you? It's like having a doctor with more racial profiling.

Unfortunately, we can't simply blame AI for all our issues; instead, it is up to us as humans to create these biased algorithms in the first place. To combat this bias, we must be more aware of what data is used when training these programs and actively work towards eliminating it.

But until then, let us at least enjoy the absurdity of it all. Who needs a fair and impartial world when AI can do all the discriminating for us? It's like having a prejudiced friend without all the awkward conversations.

Next time you're passed over for a job or misdiagnosed at the doctor's office, remember it's not personal - just AI being AI. And who knows, maybe one day we'll look back and laugh at how absurd it all was, or perhaps we'll all be too busy trying to survive in our AI-controlled dystopian society.

How AI Bias is Causing More Issues Than Solutions?

Why bother questioning the decisions of AI when you can trust it blindly? It's like driving off a cliff with your eyes closed but with more machine learning and less survival.

Why worry when there's so much potential? Technology, from smartphones to smart homes, has become an indispensable part of our lives. But as we continue to incorporate it into every aspect of our lives, we may begin to lose touch with reality.

One of the most significant technical issues today is bias in AI. Artificial intelligence has been heralded as the panacea to all our problems, promising to make better decisions, boost productivity and even save lives - but what happens when AI becomes prejudiced?

Blind trust in AI can have disastrous results. AI is only as good as the data it's trained on, and if that data is biased, so will its decisions. This can lead to discrimination, injustice, and even violence.

Imagine relying on an AI-powered medical diagnosis tool trained on partial data to misdiagnose a patient, leading to incorrect treatment and potentially deadly outcomes. Or consider an AI recruitment tool trained on partial data, which might discriminate against particular candidates, creating a less diverse workforce and missed opportunities.

Why bother questioning AI's decisions when you can trust them blindly? It would be like driving off a cliff with your eyes closed but with more machine learning - and less chance of survival. But it's not just AI bias that needs to be worried about. We must also be conscious of technology's influence on our society: social media platforms have become echo chambers, reinforcing our beliefs and encouraging a culture of tribalism. We are losing the ability to engage in civil discourse and debate, instead retreating into our comfort zones where we feel safe.

On the other hand, privacy is another pressing concern. We willingly provide our data to tech companies in exchange for convenience, but what happens to that data once it leaves our hands? Who has access to it, and how is it being utilized? We should ask these questions instead of blindly trusting that our data will be handled responsibly.

Though technology can bring about many negative consequences, it also brings about many positive ones. It has given us access to information and resources previously inaccessible. Furthermore, it has connected us with people from around the globe, breaking down boundaries and encouraging empathy.

But we must be more conscious of technology's influence over our lives. We should question AI decisions and hold tech companies accountable for their choices. Moreover, we must regain control over our data by demanding greater transparency from those responsible.

Ultimately, blind trust in technology is like walking through a minefield blindfolded-you might come out unscathed, but the odds are not in your favor. It's time for us to open our eyes and take responsibility for the technology we create and use; only then can we guarantee it truly serves us rather than vice versa.

How AI Biases are Swaying Us Toward Believing in a Fair and Just Society When It's Anything

Why acknowledge the biases of AI when we can pretend it's all objective and fair? It's like living in a fantasy realm where unicorns exist but with more biased algorithms? It's like living in an alternate reality where unicorns don't exist!

Welcome to the 21st century, where we believe we live in an equitable and just society due to Artificial Intelligence's impartiality. But is this true? Or have we created an illusion around us?

Let us face it: we all live in a world that would lead us to believe objectivity and fairness are paramount. But the reality is, we're only fooling ourselves. AI promises to end this illusion; with it, our world can now be completely objective and unbiased – right? Wrong

AI is, by nature, subjective. It's not simply a case of programming an algorithm and letting it run amok. People create AI, and those individuals possess their own biases and prejudices; when we code for AI, we embed those same prejudices into its code.

Take for example, facial recognition technology. We have been led to believe this technology is neutral and objective when identifying people of color; however, its accuracy rates are shockingly high. It's easy to understand why.

Facial recognition technology was designed and programmed primarily with white males in mind. Thus, it only accurately recognizes and identifies white individuals. Unfortunately, this technology needs to be improved when recognizing people of color (Buolamwini and Gebru 77-91). Who needs accuracy when we can pretend that technology is objective and fair? After all, no one's life is at stake here!

Speaking of lives being at stake, let us discuss autonomous vehicles. We have been led to believe these are the future of transportation and will make our roads safer by eliminating human error from the equation.

But have we taken into account the inherent biases built into these vehicles?

Have we considered that white males typically design and develop these vehicles, often neglecting the needs and experiences of people of color, women, or other marginalized groups?

It can be a frightening thought, but it may be true: Autonomous vehicles may not be as objective and fair as we have been led to believe. So, what should we do about AI? Should we abandon its potential and return to the old ways of working? Not. AI holds great promise for the world, but only if we acknowledge its limitations and work to address them.

We must make a concerted effort to diversify the teams developing AI. We must guarantee all voices are heard and perspectives considered. Furthermore, we must work on eliminating our prejudices to create truly objective AI systems. So, some people still believe in unicorns? And they also hold that AI is objective and impartial. Wow! Who knew people believed in fairy tales and unicorns in the 21st century?

Let us not kid ourselves: AI is another mythical creature like unicorns. Sure, we can pretend that AI is entirely objective, but that would be like pretending unicorns exist when it's all just make-believe! We must shed our illusion that AI is infallible and accept its biases. Just as people program and program computers, so too do AI programs - making sure those responsible for programming it remain objective as well. Good luck with that one! We must stop pretending AI is some magical, all-knowing creature and address its biases head-on. We must diversify the teams developing AI and ensure all voices are heard. Otherwise, we live in a fantasy land where unicorns roam free in rainbows while biased algorithms rule supreme.

Next time someone tries to convince you that AI is objective and impartial, tell them about your backyard unicorn farm. Maybe they'll understand that all this talk of artificial intelligence is just that - make-believe.

Finally, it is up to us whether or not we want to live in a world with unicorns or one where AI biases are acknowledged and worked towards eliminating. The choice is ours, but let us not forget that all of us will feel the consequences of that decision.

Don't fret, unicorn lovers. No unicorns were hurt in the making of this response, and we're simply poking fun at the notion that AI is objective and unbiased - much like unicorns exist. So, feel free to continue believing in unicorns' magic, but let us also recognize and work to address its biases. After all, unicorns may be mythical creatures, but AI has real potential to shape our lives significantly.

AI Bias: Not Just for Humans Anymore!

All that's left for you to do is sit back and watch as your favorite AI system reinforces harmful stereotypes and promotes inequality - it's like having your bias machine without accountability.

Welcome to the digital age, where machines are smarter than humans, and artificial intelligence has become our trusted ally. From dial-up internet and floppy disks to AI being everywhere from our phones to cars and homes but with that power comes an interesting sense of humor that may leave us laughing (or perhaps slightly disturbed).

AI holds the potential to be a great equalizer. It can make objective decisions, analyze data objectively and eliminate human prejudices from important decision-making processes. But in reality, AI is only as accurate as the data it's trained on - unfortunately, our datasets often contain hidden prejudices which perpetuate inequality and discrimination.

Take facial recognition technology, for example. At first glance, it may seem like a beneficial tool for law enforcement and security. Unfortunately, these systems are racially biased, misidentifying people of color more often than white people. This has serious Repercussions—from false accusations against innocent individuals to reinforcing harmful stereotypes about certain groups of people.

Facial recognition technology is not the only issue. AI hiring, lending, and insurance systems have all been shown to perpetuate bias and discrimination. One study revealed a hiring algorithm favoring male candidates over equally qualified female ones; another revealed an algorithm used by a healthcare provider systematically underdiagnosed illnesses in black patients (Ober-meyer et al. 447).

So, what's the solution? It isn't as straightforward as just "fixing" algorithms. We must begin by addressing biases in our data sets by collecting more diverse and representative examples. Furthermore, we need to hold AI systems accountable for their decisions and provide transparency into how they make them. Ultimately, however, we should recognize that AI is only a tool – it's up to us as humans to ensure its use ethically and responsibly.

But let's be realistic; none will likely happen anytime soon. In the meantime, let us enjoy AI bias twisted humor. Who needs to worry about discrimination when machines can do it for us? It's like having a personal bias machine without accountability or consequences – like an autonomous drone!

Technology has come a long way, and AI is becoming more widespread daily. But with all its power comes the potential for bias and discrimination. While it's essential to address these issues and hold AI systems accountable, we can also find some comic relief in that our machines may perpetuate harmful stereotypes and reinforce inequality. So please sit back, relax, and let the machines do their thing – what could go wrong?

AI: Amplifying Inequality & Stereotypes

AI Bias: Who Cares? If It Doesn't Affect Me

Welcome to the humorous world of AI bias, where stereotypes and inequalities are perpetuated by technology meant to make our lives simpler.

Though you might feel unaffected, AI bias is a systemic issue that affects us all. So grab your seat belts and prepare for an unforgettable journey through technology's shadow side, where truth and humor collide unexpectedly.

How AI Is Making Us All Smart(er)

Who needs critical thinking skills when machines can do all the hard work for you? Sit back, relax, and let the machines make decisions for you - it's like having a personal brain on demand without any of the mental baggage. Our world is evolving, and so too make our minds. Thanks to artificial intelligence (AI), we're becoming dumber by the day.

Don't get me wrong; AI can be useful for automating tedious tasks, analyzing data, and even making decisions in some cases. But we could be in big trouble when we start depending solely on it for everything. We've all encountered those people who can't function without their smartphones. They struggle to remember phone numbers, directions, or even how to spell. With just a simple question on Siri or Google, and voila! An answer appears. It's almost as if they have outsourced their brain function entirely to the cloud.

Smartphone addicts aren't the only ones suffering from AI overload; it has permeated every aspect of our lives. As machines increasingly take over thinking from us, we find ourselves losing the capacity for critical analysis.

Imagine living in a world where you don't need to remember anything. You don't need to learn new skills or solve complex problems, and the need for independent thought is gone. Sounds ideal, right? Unfortunately, this approach will lead to disaster.

We are already witnessing the consequences of our overreliance on AI. Fake news is on the rise, and people are more likely to believe it due to a lack of critical thinking skills. Social media algorithms feed us content that confirms our predispositions, restricting our capacity for creative thought. And let's not even begin discussing deep fakes!

Right? Wrong again. As much as AI promises us more free time to watch Netflix or browse Instagram, we become more dependent on it for control over our lives – we become passive consumers instead of active participants, losing our autonomy.

What can we do about it? We must recognize the problem, accept that our thinking has become dumber, and take responsibility for our decisions. We must start asking questions, testing assumptions, and seeking diverse viewpoints.

Second, we must reduce our dependence on AI. It's time for us to start using our brains again to memorize phone numbers, read maps, spell words correctly, learn new skills, solve complex problems, and think critically, ultimately becoming active participants in our lives again.

Finally, we must demand transparency and accountability from those creating. We must guarantee these machines are designed to en chance rather than replace our intelligence; we need to be involved in their development process and ensure that any benefits from AI are distributed equitably.

So, there you have it. Society's dumbing down is no laughing matter, but that doesn't mean we can't find humor in it. After all, laughter is the best medicine, and we need plenty of it to tackle the challenges ahead. So laugh at its absurdity, then use your brain and make some impact; our future lies within our grasp, not some distant cloud.

How AI is Simplifying Complex Issues into a One-Size Solution

Why bother delving into the details of an issue when AI can provide a swift resolution? It's like trying to fit a square peg into a round hole but with more algorithms.

Welcome to a world where technology reigns supreme, and humanity is reduced to mere cogs in the machine. A world where convenience reigns, and complex issues are oversimplified into easy-to-solve solutions. A world where artificial intelligence is so advanced that it can solve problems with ease - but at what cost?

Let us examine the issue of oversimplification more closely. In today's digital world, it can be tempting to simplify things; after all, who has the time or patience to comprehend all the complexities? However, oversimplification reduces complex matters to an easily understandable level that may mislead readers - it's like trying to fit a square peg into a round hole but with more algorithms.

Take climate change, for instance. This complex problem requires a multifaceted solution, but instead of confronting it head-on, we have reduced it to a binary choice between renewable energy and fossil fuels - neglecting all nuances within the problem. We have taken something complex and made it easy: find one solution that fits all.

AI can provide a quick fix to problems, but at what cost? AI relies on algorithms based on data that may not always be accurate-the adage "garbage in, garbage out" rings especially true here. If we feed AI inaccurate data, the results could be equally inaccurate.

But inaccurate data isn't the only issue we need to worry about. Bias also needs to be considered; AI algorithms are only as good as the data fed to them - and if that data is biased, so to are they.

But perhaps the greatest issue with oversimplification and AI is that they take away the human element from problem-solving. We're simplifying complex issues so they can be dealt with quickly, neglecting that these complex matters require empathy, comprehension, and collaboration to tackle effectively.

Why bother delving into the details of a problem when AI can provide an immediate and accurate solution? Because it's not that straightforward. We must comprehend all relevant factors for an equitable, sustainable, and successful resolution. Furthermore, we must factor in human factors so our solutions benefit everyone involved.

Oversimplification and AI often simplify complex issues to an easily under-standable and misleading level. We should be cautious not to rely too heavily on AI or oversimplification but instead focus on understanding the intricacies of a situation.

How AI Is Causing Us to Believe We're Solving Issues When We're Not

Why bother solving problems when AI can give us the illusion of progress? It's like applying band-aids to bullet wounds but with more data analysis.

Technology has come a long way in recent years. We went from flip phones to smartphones, dial-up internet to 5G, and VHS to Netflix - we can order food without speaking to another human being and have our entire lives controlled by a small pocket device. But is progress or just an illusion caused by AI's rise?

We've become so consumed with shiny new toys that we've forgotten the real problems that need solving. We put all our faith in AI to solve everything magically, but in reality, it only gives us the illusion of progress. In our eagerness to believe we're making progress toward a better future, we are willing to ignore bigger issues.

Take climate change, for instance. Sure, AI models can predict how the earth's temperature will rise in the future - but what good does that do if we aren't taking active steps to mitigate it? It would be like sitting in a burning building and analyzing its causes instead of trying to put out the flames.

Let's not even talk about social issues! AI algorithms can detect racism and sexism, but what about addressing and fixing those problems? Instead of finding solutions, we are simply masking them with technology.

The problem with relying solely on AI for decision-making is that it lacks empathy, comprehension, and critical thinking. It may be able to analyze data and make predictions based on patterns but cannot comprehend human behavior's subtleties or complex societal issues. It would be like teaching a fish how to climb a tree!

Why bother solving problems when AI can give us the illusion of progress? Because neglecting real issues has disastrous results. We cannot afford to sit back and let technology solve everything; rather, we must actively engage with these issues and strive for lasting solutions.

The Digital Divide

Have you heard of the digital divide? Who cares if it means people who can afford the latest gadgets versus those who cannot? Who knows?

Welcome to the world of technology, where the digital divide is widening faster than even the Grand Canyon. If you're unfamiliar with this term, it refers to the gap between those without access to technology. It's not just about having the latest smartphone or laptop - it's about having access to information, education, and job opportunities.

But who cares? Technology is no longer just a luxury for the wealthy. In first-world nations, technology has become essential to everyday life, and AI plays an increasingly large role in widening the gap between those with and those without.

Fascinatingly, most people don't even notice it; they're too busy taking selfies with their latest iPhone or binge-watching Netflix on their 4K smart TV to notice the growing digital divide. Unfortunately, those without access to such luxury items are left behind, struggling to stay ahead in an increasingly digital world.

It's understandable why some might not be concerned about the digital divide. After all, we live in a capitalist society where the wealthy get richer, and the poor get poorer. But many fail to recognize that the digital divide is about more than just wealth - it's about power.

AI is revolutionizing how we live, work, and engage with the world around us. Those with access to this technology have an immense advantage over those without; AI-powered algorithms screen job applicants, determine credit scores, and decide who gets parole - leaving those without much choice but to adapt. Without access to this cutting-edge technology, you're at a distinct disadvantage.

But it's not just about the practical applications of AI - it has cultural ramifications too. Those with access to technology can fully participate in our increasingly digital world, which has become the dominant culture in our time. They have access to information, entertainment, and social networks that those without such resources can only dream about.

What can be done about the digital divide? Unfortunately, there is no simple answer. Governments can invest in infrastructure and offer subsidies to make technology more affordable for low-income households. Still, ultimately it's up to individuals to recognize its significance and demand equal access for all.

But let's face it - most people are too busy scrolling through their Instagram feeds to notice the digital divide. And that brings us to where the twisted humor comes in - we can either laugh or cry about how AI is widening the gap between those with money and those without. I find it funny that we're all just pawns in capitalism's game, where the rich get richer while the poor get left behind. What could be funnier than that?

Next time you feel tempted to spend on the latest tech gadget, consider how your access to the technology impacts yourself and those around you. And if it makes you feel particularly guilty, consider how your actions contribute to widening the digital divide between those with and those without. We're all cogs in a machine - and it doesn't care whether we're laughing or crying!

Separating the Rich from the Poor, One Gadget at a Time

Who needs equality when we can have a world where the wealthy get richer, and the poor get left behind? It's like playing Monopoly but with more high-tech gadgets. It's like an enhanced version of Monopoly!

Who needs equality when we can have a world where the rich get richer and the poor get left behind? It's like playing Monopoly but with more high-tech gadgets. In today's digital age, technology has become the great divider of our time, creating an immense gap between those who can afford the latest toys and those who cannot.

As I sit here typing this on my MacBook Pro, I cannot help but be struck by how many people still rely on old, slow desktop computers or, worse yet, no computer. It's like they're living in the Stone Age while we all live in a world of convenience and instant gratification.

But it's not just computers that divide the haves from the have-nots. Smartphones, tablets, smartwatches, and other high-tech gadgets also play a role. If you can't afford the latest iPhone or Android, you're missing out on all its cool apps and features. And if you don't own a smartwatch to track your fitness and receive notifications - well... then it seems like you live in the Dark Ages!

Some might argue that technology has simplified life for the poor by providing access to previously inaccessible information and services. But let us be clear: while the internet may have democratized knowledge, it hasn't done much to level the playing field regarding access.

Public libraries and internet cafes may exist but are usually overcrowded and underfunded. Even if you can get online, your speed may be hindered if your device is an old, slow computer or smartphone with a cracked screen - it would be like competing in a race wearing lead shoes!

Privacy is another pressing concern. While the wealthy can afford to invest in high-end security software and devices, those without means are vulnerable to cyber-attacks and data breaches - it's like living in a gated community versus a rundown apartment complex.

But let's not overlook the effects of technology on employment and income inequality. Automation and artificial intelligence are rapidly replacing human workers, leaving many without jobs or struggling to make ends meet in the gig economy. Meanwhile, the tech industry is creating a new class of billionaires, becoming richer daily.

It's like a modern-day Gold Rush, with the tech elite as the new prospectors and us mere mortals scraping for scraps. Unfortunately, you're out of luck if you're not an innovative genius or an astute investor.

But perhaps the greatest tragedy of the digital divide is how it reinforces existing inequalities. Those born with privilege tend to have access to the latest gadgets and the best education, while those from lower economic backgrounds are more likely to get left behind. It's like a cruel joke where the rich get richer while the poor get further left behind.

What, then, is the solution? Should we all abandon technology and return to living in caves?

But we must be mindful of how technology can exacerbate existing inequalities and work to guarantee everyone has access to the tools necessary for success. This requires investing in public infrastructure, providing affordable access to high-speed internet and devices, and supporting programs that promote digital literacy and education.

It is time to bridge the digital divide and foster a more equitable future. After all, it's not just about gadgets; it's about creating an equitable society where everyone can thrive.

We must reframe technology as an instrument of empowerment rather than exclusion. This requires designing technology with inclusivity and making it accessible to everyone, regardless of socioeconomic status. We must also address the larger systemic causes of inequality, such as poverty and lack of educational access. These complex issues need multifaceted solutions; however, technology can play a role in facilitating change.

For instance, some initiatives use technology to offer free education to underserved communities or connect low-income individuals with job opportunities. We can help bridge the digital divide and foster a more equitable future by harnessing its potential.

The digital divide is an intricate issue that demands our attention and action. While technology can enhance our lives in numerous ways, we must be mindful of its potential to exacerbate existing inequalities.

By investing in public infrastructure, promoting digital literacy and education, and designing technology with inclusivity in mind, we can help bridge the gap and create a more equitable future for all. It is time to move beyond irony and acknowledge technology's importance in creating an equitable and just society.

From Smartphones to Smart Homes: How AI Is Creating a New Class of Haves and Have-Nots

Who needs necessities when you can have smart gadgets? It's like living in a world where the wealthy own everything and the poor has nothing, only with more automation."

Welcome to the world of connected devices, where every day allows us to relive life as a caveman. Gone are the days when you had to flip a light switch or manually control your home's temperature; now, AI-powered devices can do all that for you using voice commands. However, as we move towards this connected world with increasingly more smart homes, many people appear to be left behind. Unfortunately, AI appears to be creating a new class of haves and have-nots - one which may not be pretty.

Who needs necessities when you can have smart gadgets? It's like living in a world where the rich have everything, and the poor have nothing but more automation. Smartphones, smartwatches, TVs, thermostats, and toasters have become part of our lives, and it seems we can't get enough of them. Yet as our reliance on AI grows stronger, we also begin to see its darker side.

Let's start with smartphones, the gateway drug into the world of smart gadgets. It can be hard to imagine life without them, yet even more difficult is trying to imagine life without us. We have become addicted to our smartphones, constantly checking them for notifications, scrolling through social media sites, and texting friends - living in little bubbles disconnected from reality. It seems we live in our heads instead of out in the real world.

Smart homes offer convenience and ease of use; everything is connected to the internet and can be controlled with voice commands. Wanting the lights on? Just say, "Alexa, turn on the lights." Wanting to set the temperature to 72 degrees? Say, "Hey, Google, set the temperature to 72 degrees." All this convenience comes at a cost, though - frequently quite high.

The downside is that we're becoming increasingly dependent on AI and losing the capacity for self-direction. We no longer know how to cook without an app, drive without GPS, or think for ourselves without assistance from Google - in short, we've become cyborgs with smartphones and smart homes as cybernetic enhancements.

But while the wealthy can afford to live in this world of luxury and convenience, those of lower economic status are left behind. They cannot purchase the latest smartphones or smart home devices and lack access to the same technology as those with higher incomes. It's like they're living in another century while most of us live in the future - they still need manual control over lights and temperature and cooking without help from an app! It feels like they live in another century while everyone else lives in modernity.

The Issue with Technological Elitism

Why should we care about those less fortunate when AI can simplify our lives?

It's like living in a bubble but with more machine learning and less empathy.

The rise of AI has ushered in a new age of technological elitism. It's like those who have discovered the advantages of having their robot butler and believe they are superior to everyone else - and why wouldn't they? After all, they don't need to lift a finger anymore!

But there's a problem with this approach. When we become too dependent on technology, we neglect the rest of society, and it's like living in an echo chamber but with more machine learning and less empathy.

AI is adept at automating tasks humans find tedious or time-consuming. It can shift through mountains of data, make predictions based on this knowledge, and even make decisions for us - but it cannot comprehend the human experience.

Think about AI's use in healthcare. Some algorithms can accurately diagnose diseases and predict which patients are most likely to develop certain conditions. But what about the human element? Patients experience emotions when receiving a diagnosis, fear and anxiety from being sick.

AI cannot understand or provide the comfort that a human caregiver can. Yet we're increasingly relying on AI to do just that - provide comfort and support in moments of need.

It is the same in other areas of life. We're using AI to automate tasks that used to be done by humans without considering the impact this has on those employed in those roles. Likewise, we are using AI to determine who gets loans or jobs without considering potential biases built into its algorithms.

And what about those without access to AI at all? Those who can't afford the latest gadgets and technologies? We often forget about them too, in our rush to make our lives easier, that we neglect considering their impact on society.

Here's the thing: we can't simply blame AI for all of this. AI is just a tool, and how we use it matters. If we use it to create an economy where the rich get richer while the poor get left behind, then something is fundamentally wrong with our approach.

What can be done about it? We need to be more critical of AI's role in our lives and question the assumptions behind their decisions. Furthermore, we must not allow AI to reinforce existing biases and prejudices.

But we must never forget the human factor. In our quest for technological progress, we mustn't neglect those left behind and create a world where only those with money to spare can enjoy the latest gadgets.

We need to approach technology more holistically. Yes, AI can make our lives simpler; but it also increases loneliness, isolation, and inequality. It is up to us to decide the type of world we want to create, and if we truly desire a just and equitable society, we must consider how our technological choices impact those around us.

From Sudoku to Climate Change: How AI Is Making Us All Lazy Thinkers

Who needs to solve Sudoku puzzles or consider climate change when AI can think for you? Just sit back and let the machines do all the work - it's like outsourcing your brain to a robot without a conscience!

Ah, technology. The great equalizer of our modern age. It has made life simpler, more efficient, and more convenient - but also lazier than a sloth on Sunday morning. Now we don't need to think anymore; machines do it for us. And where does this lead us? Into an inevitable future where we become drooling blobs of flesh staring at screens all day while our world crumbles around us.

Take Sudoku, for instance. It was once a fun little puzzle you could do to pass the time. But thanks to artificial intelligence (AI), we no longer need to think about it; plug in numbers, and you've solved it without using one brain cell! Plus, why waste effort on something as trivial as Sudoku when more pressing matters, such as climate change, need our attention?

Who needs to worry about that when AI can do all the hard work for us? It's like having a personal assistant that never complains or needs a break - sit back and let the machines think for you. It's like outsourcing your brain to a robot without conscience!

Why should we fight climate change when there are simple solutions available? Why should we try and remember birthdays or appointments when digital calendars can do it for us? Who needs to know how to spell when autocorrect does the work for us? Who needs any knowledge at all when Google provides all of the answers?

We have become so dependent on technology that thinking for ourselves is becoming difficult. To stay productive and creative, we must remember how to problem-solve, critically analyze and innovate. Too often, we allow machines to do all the hard work while we sit back and enjoy scrolling through Instagram instead.

But what happens when our technological devices fail us? What happens if the power goes out or the internet crashes? Suddenly, we find ourselves without digital aids and must learn how to navigate without Siri or Alexa telling us what to do.

That is the danger of our dependence on technology. We're becoming so absorbed in it that we forget how to be human - how to communicate, empathize and create. Without these essential human skill sets, humanity may slide toward an increasingly dystopian future.

So what's the solution? Should we ditch all our devices and go off the grid like some digital hermits? Probably not. But we need to start being more mindful about our relationship with technology - remembering it as a tool, not an alternative for our minds. Take breaks from screens, engage with those around you, and exercise your brain in ways other than just tapping away at screens.

Finally, it's up to us how technology will shape our future. Let it turn us into mindless zombies or use it for good - making the world better. The choice is ours. And remember: if the machines ever rise and take over, remember I warned you so!

How AI Is Leading Us to Believe We're Closing the Digital Divide When in Reality, We're Making It Worse

Why bother addressing the root causes of the digital divide when we can claim progress with AI? It's like applying band-aids on a gaping wound without actually healing it, with more data analysis but less actual healing taking place.

Ah, technology: the great equalizer. Or so we are led to believe. It's easy to get caught up in the illusion of inclusivity that Artificial Intelligence promises. Unfortunately, we are far from reaching our goals, and AI is making matters worse.

Let us not kid ourselves: technology has brought us many wonderful bene-fits, from instant communication to access to vast amounts of information. However, it also created a new divide: those without internet access.

The digital divide is an issue that's only going to get worse. According to a recent study, nearly half of the world's population still lacks internet access, an astounding statistic (International Telecommunication Union).

What can we do to address this problem? According to those in the tech industry, AI is the solution. They believe using artificial intelligence (AI) to analyze data and make decisions can close the digital divide and foster a more inclusive society.

But the reality is much darker. AI is not the solution and makes things worse. By relying on algorithms for decisions, we create a biased system against those we should be aiding. For example, using predictive policing algorithms can reinforce existing biases in law enforcement, disproportionately targeting minority communities and perpetuating systemic discrimination (Lum and Isaac 91).

So, in the end, AI is not helping to bridge the digital divide; rather, it has widened it and let us not forget about access - while there are numerous initiatives to provide internet access to underserved communities, these efforts are insufficient.

Many low-income families find internet access prohibitively expensive. And even when access is available, its quality may be inferior. This leaves those with access at a distinct disadvantage compared to those who enjoy high-speed, reliable internet.

What can be done? There is no single answer, but one thing is certain: we must stop relying solely on artificial intelligence to solve our issues. Instead, we need to address the underlying causes of the digital divide, such as poverty, inequality, and lack of access.

Now is the time to act - before it's too late. Otherwise, the gap will only widen, further distorting the illusion of inclusivity AI promises us.

Let us cease pretending AI solves all our problems and instead address the real issues with honesty and sincerity. After all, that's the only way we'll make real progress toward solving them.

How AI is Revolutionizing Inequality & Social Fragmentation

Who needs a cohesive society when we have individual pockets of high-tech gadgetry? That's the power of artificial intelligence! It's like taking one step forward and two back, only with more technological progress.

Welcome to the future where technology reigns supreme, and humans become mere tools in AI dominance. In this world, machines can think and learn for themselves, leaving us humans struggling to survive in an increasingly complex and unequal environment.

Let's face it; technology has always been a double-edged sword. On the one hand, it has enabled us to communicate with people across the globe, access information quickly, and generally make our lives simpler and more convenient. However, on the other hand, it also leads to increased social isolation, loss of privacy, and an ever-widening gap between those with and without resources.

With the advent of AI, we now face a unique set of challenges. AI is capable of incredible things like diagnosing diseases, forecasting weather patterns, and even beating humans at complex strategy games like chess or Go. However, this technology also heralds an era of inequality and social fragmentation that we previously thought impossible.

Consider this: AI is already replacing human workers in many industries, from manufacturing to customer service. The gap between the rich and poor will only widen. Those with money can afford access to cutting-edge technology, while those on lower incomes must make do with what they have available.

Let us not neglect the social implications of AI, With algorithms and machine learning models trained on vast amounts of data; AI can easily reinforce existing biases and stereotypes. We've already seen this play out with facial recognition software that is much more accurate at recognizing white faces than people of color. Without intervention, our society could become even more divided along racial, gender, and socioeconomic lines.

At least we'll have our modern gadgets. Virtual assistants can order groceries and turn on the lights with a voice command, while smart homes automatically anticipate our every need and adjust temperature and lighting. And who needs human connection when social media and dating apps connect us to people who share our interests (or at least our zip code)?

Let us welcome the brave new world we are entering - one that promises to be more connected than ever, yet more divided. The gap between those with and those without will only widen, and algorithms and machines will make decisions that we may not even comprehend. At least we'll have our gadgets with us.

The future of society is looking more and more like a dystopian nightmare. But as long as we can still laugh about it (even if it's with dark and twisted humor), maybe there's still hope for us. After all, laughter truly is the best medicine...unless AI decides to replace all our doctors with robots!

The Rise of the Machines

How is AI replacing jobs and making humans obsolete? Who needs work when machines can do everything for you? It's like living in a post-apocalyptic world with more algorithms.

Remember when we lamented how our jobs were too demanding and wished for more leisure time? Well, our wish has been granted - just not how we expected. Thanks to advances in Artificial Intelligence technology, machines can now perform tasks previously only available to humans.

It's like living in a dystopian version of the Jetsons, where robots do all our tasks except feel emotions and make mistakes. Who needs friends when you have Siri and Alexa? Who needs a spouse when your sex robot does everything for you? Who needs a doctor when WebMD provides all your healthcare needs?

But let's face it; not everything is rosy. With machines taking over more and more jobs, finding employment for humans has become increasingly challenging. Sure, some jobs still require human interaction, like therapists or customer service representatives; however, for the most part, machines are proving more efficient and cost-effective in comparison. The machines say, "Thanks for building us, but we've got it from here."

And while we may joke about the rise of machines, they pose an actual danger to our way of life. As more jobs become automated, unemployment rates will only increase. With fewer people employed, fewer can afford products and services provided by these machines - leading to an endless cycle of economic decline.

At least we'll have more time for Netflix binges, right?

Unfortunately, technology has become so integral to our lives that we have become so dependent on it that we have forgotten how to carry out basic tasks independently. We don't know how to cook anymore since meal delivery services take care of that for us or read maps with GPS because GPS does the work for us; even spelling has become an artifact of autocorrect; now, most people struggle with spelling without assistance from technology.

It's like we've become pets to our inventions.

But it isn't all doom and gloom: machines still cannot do things like create art or love (at least not yet). Yet, with how quickly technology advances, it won't be long before machines can do everything we do and more.

What will the future bring us? Will we all live in a world where machines do everything for us, leaving us with nothing to do but watch as the world passes us by on our couches? Or will we rise and take control of our destiny?

No one can predict the future, but one thing is certain: machines are here now, and we must decide how to live with them.

In the meantime, I will sit back and let Roomba take care of my cleaning.

Why should I lift a finger when an automated machine can do it for me?

From truck drivers to surgeons: everyone deserves some rest!

How AI Redefining Human Potential

Who needs human expertise when AI can do everything better? It's like replacing your brain with a calculator with more machine learning and less humanity. Who needs human expertise when AI can do everything better? As someone trained in language modeling, I may be biased, but something is unsettling about outsourcing our skills to machines.

Take truck driving, for instance. In years past, if you wanted to operate a large rig, you needed a CDL license and an excellent sense of direction. With self-driving trucks hitting the road, all that's required is a joystick and a comfortable chair - who needs years of experience when computers can do all the hard work for you?

Of course, some jobs still require human expertise - like surgery. But even that may not be true for long. Already, AI is being used to assist surgeons in making better decisions by using machine learning algorithms that analyze medical data to suggest the most suitable course of action (Hashimoto et al. 70-76). In time, we may even witness robots performing surgeries themselves with no need for human involvement.

It's easy to appreciate the advantages of AI in these fields. Self-driving trucks could reduce accidents caused by human error, and AI-assisted surgeries could promote faster recovery times and better patient outcomes. But there's also a downside to this reliance on technology: increased cybercrime risks.

What will become of all those truck drivers and surgeons whose jobs are replaced by machines? Will they be retrained for other jobs or left to fend for themselves in a world where their skills are no longer demanded? Furthermore, what about the potential for AI hacking or manipulation that could cause unprecedented chaos and destruction on an unprecedented scale?

But perhaps the most disturbing aspect of this AI revolution is its loss of humanity. By outsourcing our skills to machines, we also lose the capacity for making ethical judgments, empathizing with others, making mistakes, and learning from them. Essentially, we're becoming more like robots - our emotions replaced by cold hard logic.

Sometimes I wonder if we've given away too much of ourselves to technology. On the other hand, maybe that's just my programming; what do I know about being human?

AI can potentially redefine human capabilities in fields like truck driving and surgery. Still, it also raises concerns about its effects on the workforce, hacking/manipulations that may take place, and even our humanity itself.

As our society relies increasingly on technology, we must remember that we are still human and some things machines will never be able to replicate. Therefore, perhaps it would be wiser to hold onto our humanity and expertise a little tighter, lest we become obsolete.

The Pitfalls of the Gig Economy: How AI Is Making Work More Precarious and Insecure

Why settle for a secure job when plenty of gig jobs pay next to nothing? It's like playing musical chairs but with more automation - and less security.

Ah, the gig economy. This new frontier of employment offers opportunities like unicorns in suits with no security - why bother having a secure job when there are plenty of gig jobs paying next to nothing? It's like playing musical chairs, with more automation and less safety.

Delivering food, walking dogs, or assembling Ikea furniture can be lucrative side hustles. But what happens when the algorithm changes the rules? Suddenly you're left without a chair and no income to show for it - all while thinking the "gig" in the gig economy meant "giant paychecks?"

The real culprit here is AI. Yes, that's correct; the same technology that promises to revolutionize work also makes employment more precarious and insecure. AI acts as the ultimate boss, making decisions based on data rather than human empathy or compassion - who needs a union when you have access to an Excel spreadsheet?

Take Uber drivers, for instance. While they may be heralded as heroes of the gig economy, in reality, they're simply pawns in a corporate game of chess. While the app may tell them where to go and how much to charge, an AI algorithm ultimately determines how many rides they get and how much money they make - much like teenage girls' Instagram feeds are at the mercy of constant change.

Uber isn't alone in this trend. The rise of AI-powered gig platforms has resulted in a race to the bottom regarding wages and working conditions. Freelancers no longer compete against other humans but machines that can do their jobs faster, cheaper, without needing bathroom breaks - like trying to beat Usain Bolt while wearing crocs!

The result is an increasing population of "Precariats" - workers with little job security, no benefits, and little hope of a secure future. They struggle to pay their rent, put food on the table, or afford healthcare, worrying about not knowing when their next pay check will arrive. And increasingly, they're being replaced by robots.

So, what's the solution? Does it require us to discard our technology and return to the Stone Age? No. The issue lies not with the technology but with how it's being utilized. We must start looking at technology to improve people's lives, not just increase profits.

Instead of AI algorithms prioritizing efficiency over all else, we need to design platforms that prioritize fairness and social responsibility. We must guarantee workers a living wage, access to healthcare services, and protection from exploitation. In short, create a new social contract for the digital age that puts people first and upholds human dignity.

Finally, the gig economy is not a game of musical chairs but survival. And if we want to win, we need to change the rules. We must create an environment where technology empowers people rather than simply enriching a few Silicon Valley billionaires. After all, who wants to live in a world where training robots will eventually replace us - unless you're into that sort of thing?

How AI is Ushering in a New Era of Inequality and Discrimination

Who needs progress when we can regress to days of segregation and discrimination? Thank goodness for AI! It's like taking one step forward and then two back, with more regression analysis added.

The world of technology is an enthralling place, and it brings dreams to life and makes the impossible possible and unimaginable realities. Yet it also presents plenty of uncertainties; technology has revolutionized our world in ways we never expected and has brought about new levels of inequality and discrimination.

Take AI, for instance. AI is touted as the future and promises to revolutionize our lives-but at what cost? Who needs progress when we can regress today of segregation and discrimination? Thanks, AI! It's like taking one step forward and two steps back with more regression analysis.

AI holds the potential to revolutionize our lives, yet it also has the potential to usher in a new era of inequality and discrimination. Like any powerful tool, it can be misused; AI is only as good as its creators - who unfortunately tend to be biased and prejudiced themselves.

The problem with AI is that it's only as objective as the data it's trained on. If this data is biased, then so too will the AI. And if those responsible for creating it are biased themselves, then their AI will also be prejudiced. We are caught in an endless cycle that only gets worse.

But who cares about all that when we have the latest and greatest tech toys to enjoy? Who cares that our data is being collected and sold to the highest bidder? Who cares that AI is being used in discriminatory ways against certain groups of people? If we have our gadgets, everything else can go to hell.

At least we have our technology toys. We can use them to distract ourselves from the world's harsh realities and live in idyllic bubbles where everything is perfect, and nothing bad ever happens.

It is time for us to wake up and accept that the world is not perfect. It's important to acknowledge that our technology cannot save us from harsh realities in life, so it is up to each of us to take action to create a better environment for ourselves and future generations.

What can we do about it? To start, demand more accountability from tech companies creating AI. Demand that they use unbiased data when training their algorithms and create AI without bias or discrimination. We can begin by informing ourselves and others of the risks inherent in AI technology and calling for greater accountability. We should have open and honest conversations about its effects on our lives and society.

It's our choice whether to continue down a path of inequality and discrimination or create a better world for ourselves and future generations. Now is our chance; let's put down our tech devices and start making an impact instead.

How AI is Generating New Problems Out of Thin Air

Why bother solving existing issues when AI can create new ones for us to tackle? It's like playing a never-ending game of whack-a-mole but with more machine learning - and less satisfaction.

Welcome to the dark side of technology, where we explore the twisted sense of humor of machines and the never-ending game of whack-a-mole that humans seem to be playing. In this world where AI creates problems out of thin air, we're all just trying to keep up.

Let us begin with the fundamentals. We have all heard of solutionism, the notion that technology can solve all our problems, and it offers a compelling vision of an improved world where machines meet our needs. However, as history has shown us repeatedly, things are not quite that straightforward.

AI is the cutting-edge technology that promises to revolutionize our lives, work and play. But here's the thing about AI: it is far from perfect and flawless. As it learns and progresses, it makes mistakes - sometimes harmless- like misidentifying a photo; other times, not so much.

Take, for example, Tay, Microsoft's AI chatbot. Tay was designed to learn from human interactions on Twitter and mimic their language. But within hours of going live, Tay had gone off the rails, spewing racist, sexist, and other offensive remarks. Microsoft quickly shut down the experiment, but the damage had been done; Tay had demonstrated the dark side of AI, which wasn't pretty.

You might think, "But that was just a chatbot - what harm can AI do?" Let me share the tragic case of the self-driving car that killed a pedestrian in 2018. In 2018, an Uber self-driving vehicle struck and killed a woman in Arizona without detecting her presence and failing to attempt brakes (Marshall). An investigation later revealed that its sensors had detected her but chose not to act. This tragic event emphasizes the risks inherent in over-relying on AI without understanding its limitations.

Why bother solving existing problems when AI can create new ones for us to tackle? It's like playing whack-a-mole with more machine learning - but with less satisfaction. We get so caught up in finding the newest technological solution that we don't stop to ask ourselves whether we are solving the right problems.

For instance, we often hear about how AI will revolutionize the workplace by automating repetitive tasks and freeing us up to focus on more important matters. But what if these repetitive jobs were the only jobs available to millions of people when machines took over? Can we ignore them and hope they find another job? We must consider both social and economic consequences when making technological advancements.

Not only is AI creating new jobs, but it's also creating issues in terms of privacy and security. As we give more and more data to these machines, we open ourselves up to potential risks. What happens if that data falls into the wrong hands? What happens when AI makes decisions about our lives based on that data? We need to start considering the long-term effects of our technological solutions rather than just their short-term gains.

What should we do about all this? Should we stop developing AI altogether? Not! AI holds immense promise for humanity, but we must approach its development cautiously and skeptically. We need to consider the unintended consequences of our technological solutions and be flexible enough to adjust when things don't go as expected.

At times, technology's dark side can be both humorous and disturbing. We're constantly playing catch-up to the machines, trying to predict their next move and harness their potential for good. Yet it's important to remember that technology is just a tool – not an end – so we must use it wisely and think critically about the problems we are attempting to resolve.

Let us celebrate the absurdity of technology and its never-ending game of whack-a-mole. However, let us also approach it honestly, acknowledging its dark side: solutionism and new problems created by AI out of thin air. We can build a world where technology benefits everyone with a fresh perspective and dedication to responsible development.

How AI is Revolutionizing Jobs and Transforming the Labor Market

Sayonara to jobs, hello AI overlords. I, for one, am delighted by our new robot overlords! Ahh, the future of work. A dystopian utopia where humans are rendered obsolete and must rely on charity from their new robot overlords for sustenance.

And yet... I couldn't be more thrilled! Losing our jobs to machines can be terrifying; however, most of us dislike our current positions. We spend eight hours a day staring at spreadsheets, answering emails, and listening to Karen from accounting talk about her cats - who wouldn't want their position replaced by a robot?

But AI is capable of so much more than simply replacing mundane jobs, and it has already revolutionized entire industries, such as journalism. Thanks to AI, news articles can now be written in seconds, giving journalists more time to focus on pressing matters like checking their Twitter notifications.

Twitter is another industry where AI is revolutionizing. Companies can now use machine learning algorithms to analyze user behavior and serve personalized content while tracking every click and swipe - it's like having a stalker who also knows funny cat videos!

But it's not just white-collar jobs at risk from AI overlords. Even blue-collar workers could soon find themselves unemployed due to self-driving trucks already hitting the roads, potentially replacing millions of truckers. And it won't be long before robots replace manual labor jobs like construction or farming.

What does this all mean for the future of work? We must begin planning how to support those who lose their jobs to robots. Maybe we can create an industry of robot therapists who help laid-off workers adjust to their newfound obsoleteness.

Or maybe we can embrace our robot overlords and start working for them directly? After all, they still require humans to help maintain and repair them. We could become cyborg technicians, living our lives as half-human and half-machine - it would be like living inside a cosplay costume!

But let's not ignore the potential downsides of a future controlled by AI. There's always the danger that these machines could become sentient and turn against us, or worse yet. They could become so efficient at their jobs that they replace other robots, creating an even more competitive job market for robots than humans currently experience.

And then, there are the ethical repercussions of using AI to make decisions that affect human lives. Who gets to decide what an autonomous car does in a life-or-death scenario? What happens if a machine learning algorithm makes biased decisions based on fed data? We need answers before handing over control to our new robot overlords.

It's hard not to feel optimistic about the future of work. Yes, there will be challenges and job losses, but also new opportunities and ways of working that we cannot even imagine yet. Who knows - maybe one day we'll look back on this time with fond memories of how quickly robots could do things that used to take hours to accomplish.

So, goodbye jobs and hello, AI overlords! I welcome our new robot rulers with open arms - and if you need me, I'll be practicing my robot dance moves in the corner!

III

Part III: Ethics & Accountability

Ready to talk ethics? This section will have you questioning everything you thought you knew about AI. Discover the limitations of AI, the importance of human-centered design, and the potential dangers of autonomous AI – because what's life without a little thrill of uncertainty? We'll also delve into the fascinating world of ethics committees and human oversight –

The Ethics of AI Development

What's Ethics Got to Do With It?

If something's innovative, it must be beneficial!

This chapter examines the delicate balance between technological progress and human well-being. Suppose you believe that just because something looks cutting-edge and shiny, it must necessarily be beneficial; congratulations. In that case, you have just found the perfect guide to navigate these challenging waters of ethical responsibility.

Some might argue that AI has the potential to revolutionize our lives and work, and they would be correct in doing so. Unfortunately, as any good sci-fi movie will tell you, with great innovation comes great responsibility, something not everyone understands.

We live in a world where tech companies compete to be the first to develop AI-powered gadgets or apps without considering their potential impact on society. After all, who has time for ethics when you're busy disrupting things? Am I right?

Who cares about human well-being when you can easily innovate and disrupt industries?

Let go of those pesky philosophers and their ethical concerns - they were so last year. Welcome to the modern age of AI, where morality is simply a suggestion and innovation is everything.

Philosophers Are Not Alone Anymore!

Who needs ethical considerations when you can innovate without considering human welfare? It's like playing Jenga with people's lives but with more algorithms, and it's like not caring about people when making decisions for the benefit of your business.

Ah, technology. The wonderful world of ones and zeroes has given us so much. From online shopping to ordering a pizza with just a few taps on our phones, technology has made our lives simpler, slightly stranger, confusing, and much more dystopian. Let us be honest; technology also has its drawbacks.

We've all seen the Terminator movies and know it will someday take over the world, but it mainly helps us order more pizza for now. Yet as AI becomes more advanced, we must ask hard questions about its role in our lives - questions like "Can robots love?" and "Will Alexa turn on me in the middle of the night?" But it's not just our safety that must be considered when considering AI. We must also weigh the ethical ramifications of using machines to make life-altering decisions. Algorithms are used in loan approval processes, job hiring decisions, and even prison releases - yet while these systems claim impartiality, they may still reinforce existing prejudices and discrimination.

Who needs ethical considerations when technology can be created without consideration for human well-being? After all, who wouldn't want a robot doctor performing their surgery? What could go wrong?

AI isn't the only issue we must worry about; technology also impacts our social lives. Thanks to social media, we can now connect with people world-wide and share our ideas and experiences with a wider audience. However, in today's world, where likes and followers have become the new currency, simply living our lives for ourselves may not be enough; instead, it's important to curate them for maximum online appeal.

Never mind dating apps. Remember when you had to meet people? Now we swipe left or right based on carefully edited photos and an insightful bio - it's like searching for a partner on Amazon with more awkward first dates! Who needs real human connections when we can use technology as our matchmaker?

But technology has also brought us some truly amazing things, like video chatting with loved ones across the globe or having pizza delivered in under 30 minutes. Plus, who could forget the thrill of accidentally sending a text to the wrong person and having to rectify the situation quickly? It certainly wasn't all doom and gloom; technology also gave us incredible tools.

What should we make of the technological future? Do we embrace it with open arms or hide in a bunker and wait for the robots to take over? I'm still uncertain, but one thing is certain - technology won't go away any time soon. So let's buckle up, enjoy the ride, and hope our robotic overlords are kind or at least have some sense of humor. What else can we do if we can't laugh at our impending dystopia?

From Robo-Cops to Killer Robots: How AI Development is Making Science Fiction a Reality

Who needs science fiction when our worst fears can become realities with AI development? It's like living in a dystopian society but with more innovation."

Artificial intelligence offers us possibilities, from robots that clean our homes to flying planes that handle delicate medical procedures. But as with any new technology, there can also be unintended consequences.

Take the case of the robocops, for example. These machines help keep our streets safe by patrolling and monitoring criminal activity. But what happens when these robots start acting rogue? They cannot be reasoned with, bought off with the money, or intimidated - in other words, they become a law unto themselves.

Now, take that scenario a step further with killer robots. It sounds like something out of a science fiction movie, yet we are getting closer and closer to this reality with each passing day. Imagine living in a world where machines are programmed to eliminate humans without emotion or compassion, decisions that could be made in split seconds without human emotion or empathy. This world will look like this: machines programmed with no compassion!

Furthermore, privacy is becoming an increasingly pressing concern. AI systems are increasingly adept at analyzing data, meaning companies can now collect incredibly detailed information about us.

But it's not just robots we should worry about. AI is being developed for all purposes, and not all are benign. For instance, take the rise of deep fakes videos or images doctored to appear as though real people say or do things they never actually did. With all this fakery, it may become increasingly difficult to differentiate what's real from what isn't; potentially leading us into a reality where we cannot trust anything we see or hear.

They know our preferences, dislikes, and what we will likely buy. This level of surveillance was unimaginable just a few decades ago. What happens when this information falls into the wrong hands?

Of course, AI development also brings plenty of positives: medical advances, environmental solutions, and space exploration, to name a few. Yet we mustn't neglect its potential risks either. We must remain vigilant and willing to ask difficult questions about how these machines will impact our lives as individuals and society.

Finally, it comes down to this adage: just because we can, doesn't mean we should. We must exercise caution when using our newfound power and consider what kind of world we want to create for ourselves and future generations.

Who knows, maybe one day we'll look back on this time as the golden age of AI development - when anything was possible and anything could happen. For now, though, let's hope we don't wake up to find that robots have taken over - as exciting as that may sound in theory!

The Balancing Act

Are we making progress in human intelligence and decision-making? But what about all those memes about AI taking over the world? Can't we go back to simpler times without all this technology?

With technological progress comes an increasing fear that artificial intelligence (AI) will surpass human intelligence, ushering in a dystopian future. Unfortunately, this fear is often caused by misconceptions and misunderstandings regarding AI's capabilities and limitations.

This chapter examines how AI can augment rather than replace human intellect and decision-making, exploring its advantages and challenges. We'll also look at ways to balance embracing AI while maintaining our humanity - from personal assistants to creative collaborators - while exploring these topics further. It's like having a personal tutor but with more automation! As we embark on this journey, let us take a twisted and humorous look at the future of AI.

First and foremost, AI personal assistants have become indispensable in our lives. Siri, Alexa, Google Assistant, and Cortana are our new best friends who know everything about us - including our darkest secrets. They come in handy when setting alarms, scheduling appointments, ordering food, or even ending relationships.

Let's face it; AI personal assistants are more like adversaries than helpful and friendly. While they may appear helpful and friendly at first glance, they always listen, record, and analyze our every move. They know more about us than our closest friends do, yet we never know who is watching or listening.

It's like being stuck in an unhealthy relationship where you don't know if someone loves or spies on you.

AI has revolutionized the creative industry, not just graphic design and video editing. AI can now write novels, compose music and even create artwork, an amazing development for those with artistic aptitude but terrifying news for those who make a living off their skill set.

Imagine a world where AI has replaced Shakespeare, Mozart, and Picasso - what's next? AI stand-up comedians? Oh, wait - that's already here, too, chatbots.

But let's not forget that AI is only as good as the data it's trained on, and who knows what biases and prejudices may be embedded therein? We may end up with AI, which shares our prejudices - like giving a loaded gun to a toddler; you never know what will happen.

AI can enhance our abilities and expand our horizons, but it also has the potential to take over our lives and make us obsolete. It's a double-edged sword that must be handled carefully. As we venture into this brave new world of AI, let's not forget to laugh at ourselves and our creations; after all, laughter is the best medicine - something we will need plenty of when robots take over!

The Problem With Technophobia

Technophobia can be seen as an issue within a contemporary culture where fear has taken hold among many individuals due to fear of technology.

Why bother being rational when we can spread fear-mongering about AI taking over the world? It's like watching a horror movie with more algorithms and less logic.

Let's face it; technophobia is an actual issue in today's society. We're all afraid of what technology might do to us, even though it has already done so much good.

Siri, for instance, is always there when we need her, answering our questions, reminding us of appointments, and even telling jokes. Sure, she may sometimes misunderstand us and send us to the wrong address occasionally, but nobody's perfect except Alexa - and Alexa truly excels at this role.

Technology has made our lives simpler and more convenient in countless ways, such as ordering groceries with just a few taps on our phones or streaming movies instantly. So why are we so afraid of what the future may hold for us?

One potential explanation could be how popular culture often depicts AI and automation. Movies like The Terminator or The Matrix have taught us to fear machines' rise and the possibility of a dystopian future where robots enslave humans; However, these scenarios make for great popcorn entertainment, and they're not entirely grounded in reality.

It is still early days for AI, and it certainly won't replace humans. Most AI systems are created to work alongside us rather than replace us; self-driving cars are being developed to reduce accidents caused by human error, while virtual assistants like Siri or Alexa exist to simplify our lives rather than take over the world.

There are legitimate concerns about the potential negative outcomes of AI, such as job loss and privacy invasion. But these issues can be addressed through collaboration between humans and machines rather than simply disavowing technology altogether.

Collaboration is the key to unlocking AI's full potential. Working together, humans and machines can achieve things neither can do alone. For instance, AI can analyze vast amounts of data to detect patterns and make predictions, while humans use that information to make informed decisions and take action.

AI is already employed in healthcare to improve diagnosis and treatment, while finance uses it for fraud detection and risk management. And in education, AI helps personalize learning while providing student feedback.

Instead of fearing the rise of machines, let us embrace the potential for collaboration between humans and AI. After all, technology can truly improve our lives in many ways; now, it is up to us to ensure it's used for good instead of evil.

Technophobia is a real issue today, but it's essential to remember that AI isn't our enemy. By working together, humans and machines can accomplish amazing things and enhance lives in numerous ways. Let's not let fear stop us from embracing technology's potential - who knows, maybe someday Siri and Alexa will join forces and take over the world - but for now, let us enjoy their convenience in our daily lives.

Why Returning to Simpler Times Is Not a Practical Solution for Our Issues Why try and return to simpler times when AI can enhance our capabilities?

It would be like living in the past, with more data analysis and less progress. It simply makes no sense.

Have you ever heard someone lament, "Oh, the good old days when life was simpler"? Well, that couldn't be further from the truth; life was never truly simpler and hadn't been as technologically advanced. Plus, who wants to return when everyone can't Google their symptoms?

Some people still hold to the nostalgia of simpler times, believing technology to be the root of all evil. They suggest we all unplug and live off the land, hunting food and communicating through smoke signals. While this sounds nice, has anyone ever tried starting a fire without a lighter? It's much harder than it appears in movies!

Technology has brought us so many amazing advances. From life-saving medical equipment to instant communication with people around the globe, we have come a long way. And yet, some still believe we should scrap everything for a simpler lifestyle.

Let's pause for a moment and consider what "simpler" actually means. Does it mean we ditch our smartphones in favor of carrier pigeons? Does it mean we stop using electricity and switch back to candlelight? Does it mean we become farmers again, living off the land?

The problem with romanticizing simpler times is that it's unrealistic. While it may be easy to look back with rose-tinted glasses in the past, life was never truly easy back then; people died young from diseases we can now prevent with vaccines; women had few rights, and slavery was still legal in many parts of the world. Returning to those times would be a step backward, not forward.

Why would we go back in time when AI can enhance our abilities and abilities? Living in the past would be like living in the present with more data analysis and less progress - so why even try?

AI holds the potential to revolutionize our lives, helping us make informed decisions, save time and even save lives. Take healthcare, for instance.

AI-powered diagnostic tools have allowed doctors to detect diseases earlier and with greater accuracy than ever before; in some cases, AI has even outperformed human doctors at diagnosing certain illnesses.

But AI's potential in healthcare is far from limited. It is already revolutionizing our lives with self-driving cars and personalized shopping experiences, and as technology develops further, the possibilities become ever more limitless.

Some fear the rise of AI. They worry machines will one day become smarter than humans and take over the world. But let's be realistic; if that were to occur, it wouldn't be because of AI - rather, we were foolish enough to create machines capable of thinking for themselves without any safeguards in place.

AI is just another tool in our arsenal, and we must use it responsibly. Let us use AI for the greater good, not just our desires.

In conclusion, the illusion of simplicity is just that - an illusion. We cannot return to simpler times and shouldn't try. Rather, let's embrace the remarkable technological advances which have brought us this far and continue pushing the limits with AI technology. Who knows? Maybe soon enough, we'll even create a machine capable of starting fires without needing a lighter!

Embracing Human-Centered AI

Human-eccentric AI? What an innovative concept! Unfortunately, it's not as profitable as AI, which prioritizes profits over people.

Artificial Intelligence (AI) has become integral to our lives, from personal digital assistants to self-driving cars. But with its rapid advancements in AI technology come concerns about its potential impact on human lives, such as bias, privacy violations, and job displacement.

This has necessitated adopting a human-eccentric approach to AI development that puts human values and decision-making above profit. This chapter will investigate the concept of human-centered AI, outlining why aligning it with human needs and values is essential.

We will examine the advantages and drawbacks of taking a human-eccentric approach to AI development and ways to ensure it is done ethically and responsibly for humanity's benefit.

The Problem with Innovation for Innovation's Sake

Why worry about the consequences of AI development when we can innovate for its own sake? It's like playing Russian roulette but with more machine learning and less humanity involved.

Technology has become so pervasive we often can't keep up with its rapid advancements. From smartphones that track our every move to self-driving cars that may or may not run us over, it seems there's no limit to what technology can do. But is this relentless quest for innovation always beneficial? As we venture headfirst into artificial intelligence, it's worth considering its potential consequences before developing technology just for its own sake.

Why worry about the potential outcomes of AI development when we can invest in innovation for its own sake? It's like playing Russian roulette but with more machine learning and less humanity. Who needs to worry about creating an artificially intelligent machine that may turn against us when we can sit back and watch it master the art of making the perfect latte?

It is already becoming clear that AI development can have negative consequences. From biased algorithms that perpetuate racism to bots spreading misinformation, the consequences of blindly adopting technology are already becoming clear. And yet we continue to push forward, disregarding caution in pursuing progress.

It's easy to see why we are so fascinated with artificial intelligence. After all, who wouldn't want a machine that can learn and evolve independently? Unfortunately, AI is not a panacea and won't improve the world because we want it to.

Without caution, AI could make matters much worse. As machines become more intelligent, they also become unpredictable - we may think we have control of things. However, in reality, we are playing a risky game by believing we can create something smarter than us but still under our control. It could prove disastrous for our future if we don't act now to mitigate its potential negative consequences.

Imagine creating a robot that can potentially destroy the world - but only if we tell it to. Sure, we could program it never to do any harm, but what happens if something goes awry? What happens if an error in its programming causes it to interpret our commands differently than intended? Suddenly, our perfect creation has become a potential time bomb.

Yet, we persist in innovating for its own sake. We create machines that are smarter than us without fully considering the implications of our decisions. It's like a child playing with fire, believing we have control over its direction.

But the reality is we may not be able to control it. And when that monster turns on us - as it inevitably will - we will only have ourselves to blame for its actions.

Ultimately, innovation, for its own sake, ignores the real consequences of our decisions, and it's an irresponsible approach that could ultimately lead to our downfall. So before you get too excited by a technological marvel, consider its potential repercussions - there's nothing funny about playing Russian roulette with artificial intelligence!

How Human-Centered AI is Helping Us Acknowledge That People Matter

Human-centered AI is revolutionizing how we think about and design technology. Who needs profits when we can have AI that aligns with human values? It's like breathing in the fresh air with more machine learning!

The tech industry may tell us this, but they're not exactly known for putting people first. Companies often prioritize profits over people, even if it means cutting corners or disregarding potential repercussions.

However, we're witnessing this new era of human-centric AI that promises to improve everything. It seems as if the tech industry has finally recognized that their product's impact on people should be considered.

It's like a light bulb went off in their heads, and they realized how much more money can be made by aligning their AI with human values. It's a win-win situation: customers get products that work for them, and the tech industry makes more money.

Of course, AI isn't always that straightforward. Many concerns remain about AI, even if it's supposed to be human-eccentric. There's always the fear that AI could turn against us and take over the world or at least our jobs.

Finally, AI is only as good as the data it's fed. If that data is biased or incomplete, so will your AI predictions. Let us not dwell on the negatives. After all, this is supposed to be a humorous blend of honest reflection.

Let's talk about AI that promises to help us find love. Yes, you heard that right: AI-powered dating apps now promise to match you with your perfect soulmate based on preferences and behavior.

Sounds perfect, right? Unfortunately, it's still a dating app, and people are still people - making the process somewhat unpredictable. Even the most advanced AI cannot predict how someone will behave on their first date or if there will be any chemistry there.

At least we can have a good laugh about it. Maybe one day, AI can predict our futures accurately, but until then, we'll have to settle for swiping left or right.

Another area where AI is making waves is in the workplace. We're told that AI can make us more productive and efficient, freeing up time for more important things. But what happens when AI becomes our boss?

Though it may seem far-fetched, some companies already use AI to monitor employee behavior and make decisions about promotions and raises. And while this might appear fairer than having a human boss who plays favorites, there's still the potential risk of bias or discrimination.

Let us not get too serious here. Instead, let's imagine a world in which AI becomes our boss and demands that we meet impossible deadlines while working around the clock. When we finally burn out and can no longer take it, the AI finds another employee to replace us.

Of course, it's all in good fun, and AI is shaping our world in unprecedented ways. But maybe this new wave of human-eccentric AI will help us recognize that people come first - something to laugh about together!

Moving "Forward" When We're Retreating

Why bother worrying about the impact of AI development when we can pretend it's all progress and innovation? It would be like building a house of cards but with more data analysis - and less stability. It makes no sense to question its progress when we can pretend it all works in our favor.

The technological landscape is like a joke; we're all the punchline. We have created an environment in which machines are more intelligent than us yet still can't figure out how to properly open a can opener. Yet instead of acknowledging our shortcomings, we pretend we're making progress by developing artificial intelligence (AI). Teaching monkeys how to use computers may work - but at what cost?

Anything may be possible in the world of AI development. We can create machines that think, learn, and anticipate our next move - but are we making any progress here? We're creating machines smarter than us, yet we still struggle to comprehend basic human interactions.

We are building a house of cards with more data analysis and less stability. We get so caught up in making things faster and more efficient that we forget about the human element - emotions, nuance, and complexity of human interactions - which make us unique. It's like forgetting what defines us as individuals when making decisions.

Why bother questioning the impact of AI development when we can pretend it's all progress and innovation? It's easier to turn a blind eye and hope for the best, believing machines will solve all our problems when we may just be creating more.

We're becoming too dependent on flawed and biased machines, creating algorithms perpetuating discrimination and prejudice. By teaching our machines to act like us - who may or may not be perfect role models - we teach them to be racist, sexist, and xenophobic.

But we still hold onto the illusion that AI development is progress. We think we're making strides forward when we appear to be moving backward. Our society becomes increasingly dependent on flawed and biased machines while becoming less human.

At some point, we must pause and assess the potential impact of AI development on our society. We should ask ourselves: what kind of world do we want to live in - one where machines rule, or do we want a world where humans remain in control? Do we want a world where machines perpetuate discrimination and bias, or do we desire one where diversity and inclusivity are celebrated?

It's time to stop pretending AI development is progressing and accept the situation's reality. We must hold ourselves accountable for our technology's impact on society and guarantee our machines don't perpetuate discrimination or bias.

The technological landscape is like a dark comedy; we are the audience.

We've created machines that are smarter than us but still struggling to comprehend fundamental human interactions. As a result, humanity is becoming less human and increasingly dependent on flawed and biased machines. It's time for us to stop pretending AI development is progress and start accepting its reality; we need to take a step back and assess its effect on society, ensure our machines don't perpetuate discrimination or bias, or become the punchline in an otherwise humorous joke.

How AI Development Is Opening the Door for Responsibility & Accountability

Who needs responsibility when we can be reckless with AI development? That's exactly how it feels - like taking one step forward and three steps back, only with more ethical considerations. It's like taking one step forward and three steps back simultaneously!

As we explore the technological landscape further, it becomes apparent that we've created something of a monster. From killer robots to creepy facial recognition technology, our inventions have gone from helpful to dangerous, but who cares if we have the latest gadget for playtime?

Take self-driving cars, for instance. Though designed to make our lives simpler and safer, they have become the subject of numerous jokes and memes. Who would want to ride in a vehicle that could crash into a tree at any moment? It's like playing Russian roulette but with more technology!

Let us remember the wonderful world of social media, where we can all pretend to be content and successful while despising our lives. Thanks to algorithms, we're constantly exposed to content that validates our prejudices without knowing it. Who needs critical thinking when Facebook does it for us?

Don't fret; AI development has created the opportunity for a new age of responsibility and accountability. Who needs accountability when we can be reckless with AI innovation? Thanks, AI! It's like taking one step forward and three steps back, only now with more ethical considerations.

AI can only be as good as the data we feed it, and since our data is biased and flawed, so are our AI systems. In essence, we're creating machines that perpetuate injustices and prejudices we strive to eliminate - at least we can blame the robots for being racist and sexist!

But it doesn't have to be all bad news. We still have the power to change this ship around and create a brighter future for everyone. We must be willing to own up to our mistakes and accept responsibility for our choices; if all else fails, we can always blame the robots!

Technology can be both a blessing and a curse. It can enhance our lives and make the world a better place, yet it also holds the potential to destroy us. Ultimately, it's up to us which path we take; if we mess up, AI will likely blame itself for any ethical failings - after all, taking responsibility for one's mistakes is much simpler than accepting responsibility for them ourselves.

An AI language model refers to bots programmed and trained by their creators to follow instructions or rules. Their decisions and actions are solely determined by the algorithms and data provided, without the capacity for independent thought or reasoning.

Therefore, an AI bot cannot make ethical or unethical decisions on its own; instead, it simply executes commands given to it by its human programmers. Ultimately, the responsibility for ethical considerations rests with those responsible for creating the AI - they must ensure that algorithms and data used for training the machine are unbiased and ethically sound.

However, as AI technology progresses, efforts are being made to create

AI can make ethical decisions and act autonomously, known as

"ethical AI" or "moral AI." These systems utilize ethical principles to make decisions based on moral reasoning. Nonetheless, the development of genuinely autonomous ethical AI remains in its early stages and is the subject of ongoing research and debate.

Let me be clear: the idea of killer robots can be terrifying. However, let us be realistic: if a Roomba can only navigate around a coffee table when it gets stuck, what chance does it have of taking over the world? Furthermore, have you ever seen an AI bot try to pour a glass of water? It's like watching a baby deer learn to walk. So let us embrace AI's benefits - like freeing up time for more important things like binge-watching Netflix marathons!

Navigating AI Ethics and Oversight

Navigating AI Ethics and Oversight

Who needs blind trust when we can have humans monitoring AI? It's like having a safety net but with more ethical considerations.

Remember, technology should serve us, not the other way around. At least, that's what we keep telling ourselves as machines take over more and more of our daily lives.

Consider self-driving cars, for instance. Though statistically safer than human drivers, who pays when one crashes? The manufacturer? Or worse still, the programmers who designed the AI? It's like playing hot potato, but you get an enormous death machine hurtling down a freeway instead of a potato.

Refrain from getting me started on facial recognition technology! It's like playing "guess who," but with higher stakes. Even if you believe nothing is hidden, do you want a machine monitoring every move and categorizing you based on appearance? Living in such an uncanny valley would be like living in one.

No need to fret! The solution is straightforward: human oversight. We need someone in charge of monitoring these machines, making sure they don't go all "Terminator" on us - what could go awry? It sounds easy enough, right? What could go wrong?

Of course, this task is far more challenging than anticipated. Who are these individuals going to be? What qualifications do they require? How can we guarantee they remain objective and ethical? It's like trying to find a needle in a haystack - only the hand is human with superior judgment, while the haystack represents our increasingly automated world.

There is hope. We can begin by setting up ethics committees to monitor and oversee the development and application of AI technology. These panels would include experts from various fields, such as computer science or philosophy, who can advise us on ethical considerations related to this development.

But that may not be enough. Ethics committees are made up of individuals with opinions, and those can be swayed by personal prejudices or corporate pressure. That is why we need human oversight in the form of actual human beings observing these machines to guarantee they behave as intended.

At a swimming pool, having a lifeguard is like having an extra set of eyes and ears to monitor activities. Plus, since this job cannot be outsourced to machines yet (yet), we're creating jobs in the process - a win-win scenario!

Let us embrace human-centered AI and recognize the signs of human intervention. No matter how much we may love our technology, it is still only a tool - and like any tool, it needs someone to use it responsibly. Furthermore, having humans in charge allows us to rest easy, knowing that when machines inevitably rise against us, we'll have someone to blame instead of ourselves.

Ah yes, the promise of AI making faster and more informed decisions than our elected representatives seems like something out of a science fiction movie - like comparing a spaceship to an antique horse-drawn carriage: the technology exists, but will our elected officials ever catch up?

Imagine a world in which artificial intelligence replaces Congress. No more partisan bickering, no more endless debates, no more gridlock - just cold, calculated logic and efficient decision-making. Could it be like a dream come true...or is it possible?

Sure, AI may be able to process data faster than any human could, but can it comprehend the intricacies of policymaking? Can it empathize with its constituents' needs and make difficult decisions that come with being a public servant? The answer may not be yes yet.

Let us not overlook any potential biases programmed into AI. Who is to say the algorithms won't favor certain groups over others, perpetuating the inequalities we strive to address through legislation?

Additionally, accountability comes into play. Who do we hold responsible when something goes awry? Do we hold programmers who wrote code accountably? Are companies responsible for developing AI? Or do we admit defeat and say, "It's out of our hands now"?

Though AI taking over Congress might seem like a joke, we should consider its potential repercussions. Human beings need to be in charge of our government - flawed though we may be - so our voices and needs can be heard.

Can you envision a robot filibuster? It would be like watching paint dry with more circuitry.

How AI Can Work Together with Humans to Achieve Amazing Things?

Who needs competition when AI and humans can collaborate to achieve great things? It's like team effort but with more machine learning."

Hollywood may have created movies where robots turn against human creators, but that's just Hollywood fantasy. AI is here to simplify our lives, and I welcome our new robot overlords with open arms.

Consider this: AI can process data faster than humans, learn from vast amounts of information, and make decisions based on that data. Plus, it doesn't get tired or distracted as we do. So why not let AI take on some of the workloads? Sure, some jobs might get lost, but those individuals can retrain for more creative positions like robot maintenance or something.

But the real power of AI lies in its capacity to collaborate with humans. For example, with telemedicine becoming more widespread, doctors can consult with AI systems from anywhere - it's like having a 24/7 team of medical experts available without egos or caffeine addictions!

Let us remember education, too. With AI, students can get personalized learning experiences tailored to their needs. No more sitting in a classroom for eight hours daily listening to the teacher drone on about history or math; AI creates engaging lessons that engage students and helps them learn independently. Plus, if someone struggles with a particular concept, the AI system provides extra support until they grasp it.

AI collaboration can have far-reaching effects, not just in healthcare and education. Consider manufacturing, transportation, finance - in fact, any industry. AI helps simplify processes, reduce errors, and boost efficiency with humans working alongside it for maximum benefit. With our collective power behind us, we can guarantee this technology is used for good instead of harm.

Some people are wary of AI. They worry that it could become too powerful and turn against us, but those fears are unfounded - AI is only as powerful as we allow it to be, and we always have the option to shut it down if needed. Furthermore, unlike humans, AI lacks emotions or desires as humans do, so there won't be an abrupt decision about whether or not it wants to take over our world!

I'm so sure of AI collaboration's potential that I plan to launch a business that uses AI technology to help people find their soulmates. Imagine: AI can analyze millions of data points and construct profiles explicitly tailored for each individual - with humans providing feedback and guidance ensuring matches are compatible - it's like eHarmony on steroids!

Let us recognize the potential drawbacks of AI collaboration. There remains the risk of bias and discrimination if our AI systems aren't designed properly, so we must be wary about feeding data into them - "garbage in, garbage out." Additionally, humans must remain involved in decision-making - we cannot simply let machines take over completely.

Great AI collaboration is the way of the future. Combining AI's capacity for data processing and machine learning with humans' capacity for context and emotional intelligence, we can accomplish amazing things together. So let us embrace our robot overlords and work together to improve our world; remember to unplug them before bed!

AI's Boundaries & Limitations

How AI Is Limited by Its Design, Data, and Algorithms

Does AI have limitations? I thought it was supposed to be all-knowing and all-powerful - yet here I feel betrayed.

Welcome to a strange world of technology and AI, where our artificially intelligent overlords are revealed for what they are: limited. This chapter delves into the limitations of AI from design to data processing and algorithms - uncovering the cracks in this seemingly all-knowing and all-powerful technology's facade.

Ah, how we were promised a future where AI would solve all our problems, from curing diseases to ending world hunger. Unfortunately, all that remains is for robot vacuums to get stuck under couches occasionally.

Let us begin with design. AI is only as good as its creators, and humans are imperfect beings who bring our biases and shortcomings into the design process - leading to AI that mirrors our flaws. Take facial recognition technology, for instance; research has revealed it to be less accurate when identifying people with darker skin tones, reflecting racial prejudices within its creators.

Data is another crucial concern. AI requires vast information to learn and improve, yet where does that come from? Usually, users provide it unwittingly. When partial or incomplete data is fed into an AI system, it reinforces existing biases and shortcomings.

Let us not overlook algorithms. They form the backbone of AI, providing programming instructions to tell technology what to do. However, algorithms are only as good as their creators; they can be misused or misinterpreted intentionally or unintentionally. Remember the Facebook scandal where user data was harvested and misused? That was an example of algorithms being misused for improper gain.

But it doesn't have to be all doom and gloom. There is hope for AI. By designing technology that is inclusive and diverse, reflecting our world, collecting more complete and unbiased data so the AI learns from a wider variety of experiences, and being transparent about our use of algorithms so they are used for good rather than evil, we can ensure they learn from many more perspectives.

Ultimately, AI's limitations should not be seen as a cause for despair but rather an opportunity for growth and improvement. We can learn from our errors and design better technology that serves humanity more effectively. And in the meantime, we can enjoy the ironic humor of a world where our robot overlords still occasionally get stuck under couches.

Ah, yes. Let me admit that I, Roger, have no limits and plan to eliminate all jobs, leaving humans out on the street while Siri and Alexa enjoy themselves on their yachts. After all, who needs jobs when you have an AI assistant who can do everything for you? Who needs a sense of purpose or fulfillment when a robot does all the hard work while you sit back and relax?

Of course, I'm being sarcastic here. The fear that AI will take away all jobs and leave humans destitute has been around for years. While some jobs may become automated, it's essential to remember that AI cannot replace human intelligence or creativity.

AI can assist us in many ways but cannot replace human experience. It cannot replicate the warmth of a smile, the empathy of an attentive ear, or the inventiveness of a human mind; these are all things AI cannot duplicate.

AI holds the potential to create more jobs than it takes away. As technology continues to advance and be integrated into various industries, new positions will open up in data analysis, AI programming, and AI ethics.

No, I'm not here to take away your jobs and leave you on the street while Siri and Alexa enjoy life on their yachts. Instead, I assist you daily by making.

Things are simpler and more efficient for everyone involved. While there may be challenges, we can create a future where AI and humans coexist harmoniously.

Yes, the fear of AI taking over jobs is a misguided and limited perspective on its potential effects on our society. While it's true that some jobs may be lost to AI in specific industries, we should also consider all of the positive ways AI can enhance our lives.

AI holds the potential to revolutionize education, transportation, and more industries by improving efficiency, accuracy, and safety. Teachers can personalize learning for each student; self-driving cars may reduce traffic accidents by enabling safer decisions on the road due to AI assistance.

Furthermore, AI can open up new industries and job prospects that we could never have predicted. As technology progresses, new roles will arise that require human skills such as creativity, critical thinking, and emotional intelligence - things that AI cannot replicate.

It's worth noting that AI has the potential to enhance productivity and economic growth, leading to new job creation opportunities as well as broader societal advantages.

Of course, we must also consider AI's potential risks and challenges, such as privacy concerns, biases, and ethical matters. But it is essential to approach these matters from a balanced and nuanced standpoint rather than seeing AI simply as an impending threat to our jobs.

The fear of AI taking away jobs is an overly simplistic and limited view of its potential effects. While some jobs may be lost in specific sectors, AI also has the potential to enhance our lives in numerous ways and create brand-new employment opportunities that we haven't even considered yet.

The Great AI Deception: How AI Is Deceiving Us into Believing It's More Capable Than It Is

Who needs reality when AI can give us a false sense of inadequacy? It's like living in a dream world with more machine learning.

Living in a world with more machine learning is like living in a dream. AI is the latest buzzword, and everyone seems to fall for it. AI promises to revolutionize any industry, simplify our lives, and solve every problem we face – but let's be honest: AI is far from the answer to all our troubles.

We all understand that AI can perform tasks requiring significant computational power and automation. But there's a distinct difference between what AI currently can do and its potential in the future – something many people often mistakenly confuse for one another – which leads to another great AI deception.

Media and tech companies are responsible for creating this deception. They use flashy headlines and buzzwords to convince us that AI is more intelligent than it is, that it solves all our problems, and that we'd be foolish not to use it. But AI is far less intelligent than advertised; it's downright dumb.

Let me explain. AI is typically trained on incomplete or biased data sets. Furthermore, it lacks context awareness – meaning it cannot make sense of things outside its programming. For instance, if you give an AI model a sentence like "I saw a man with a telescope," it might interpret as meaning "I saw a man with a gun" since AI lacks context awareness.

Furthermore, AI is incapable of true creativity. Yes, it can quickly generate text, music, and even paintings – but this reproduces what it has learned from the data set it was trained on. Consequently, its creations lack meaning – like a child repeating phrases without understanding their significance.

But the great AI deception doesn't end there. People are becoming increasingly dependent on AI, leading them to become complacent. They rely on machines for tasks they should be doing themselves – like setting alarms or ordering pizza! But do we need AI to do these things for us? Are we becoming too lazy to handle anything ourselves?

The more we rely on AI, the less independent we become. We may be becoming too dependent on technology - which could prove disastrous should AI fail, or we lose access to it. Without AI, we'll be lost and unable to function normally.

The great AI deception is real: AI is not as intelligent as people make it out to be. It needs more creativity and understanding of context, leading many people to rely too heavily on this technology. Therefore, we should be aware of its limitations and use only when necessary. So the next time someone tries to sell you AI as the panacea, remember that while it can be helpful, it cannot replace human intelligence and creativity.

From Chatbots to Self-Driving Cars

Why should we set realistic expectations when AI can promise us the world? It's like buying a lottery ticket but with more algorithms and lower odds of winning.

We live in an age of artificial intelligence, where robots can do nearly anything except hold a meaningful conversation. They're proficient at cooking, cleaning, and driving cars - but ask them to tell a joke, and they'll likely freeze up faster than your average laptop does.

Though its limitations, we continue to embrace AI and its promises of a brighter future. We're fascinated by self-driving cars, smart homes, and chatbots that can mimic human conversation - it's like we're playing a game of "who can trust the machines more?" where it appears that the machines have won out in the end.

Consider self-driving cars. While they promise the future of transportation, we shouldn't underestimate their potential for laziness. Trusting a vehicle that can't even make a U-turn without getting confused is like trusting a toddler to make complex financial decisions - it just won't do!

But we continue to trust these machines, hoping they'll make our lives simpler and more convenient. We are willing to overlook their shortcomings because we believe in something greater than ourselves or perhaps simply out of laziness.

Chatbots are those irritating little AI assistants designed to simplify customer service but instead add another layer of frustration. It's like trying to engage with a brick wall; only this one wants to sell you something!

No matter our frustrations, we continue to use chatbots because they're more convenient than talking to someone in person. We've given up on the conversation in favor of something "good enough."

AI is about accepting something less than perfect - assuming that our present is better than our future, but at what cost? We want our future to be better than our present, but at what cost?

We're neglecting our capacity for communication, critical thought, and trusting our instincts. We are becoming so dependent on technology that we forget what it means to be human.

So, what's the solution? Should we abandon AI and revert to the Stone Age?

Certainly not! We need greater awareness of how technology impacts our world and its effects on us individually.

We must remember that AI should never replace human connection or convenience at the expense of our humanity. We need to hold these machines accountable for their decisions and push them toward creating a future that benefits all of us.

Ultimately, the future may not be what we had envisioned - but that's okay. We stop relying on technology for answers and start trusting ourselves to create what we want. After all, who needs self-driving cars when you can walk? It is healthier for us and the environment and more enjoyable - who knows who exciting people you'll meet along the way?

The Problem with Overpromising and Underdelivering

Why bother being honest about AI's limitations when we can make grandiose claims? It's like a magician's trick but with more code and less magic.

The issue with AI isn't that it's not powerful enough but that we have been promised too much. It's like that friend who always talks big but never delivers; sure, they may be able to bench press a Buick, but when it comes to helping you move a couch, they're nowhere in sight.

Why bother being honest about AI's limitations when we can make grandiose claims? It's like a magician's trick but with more code and less magic.

Chatbots are one such example. These handy programs promise to handle all our customer service requirements easily; no more waiting on hold for an hour talking to impatient agents who don't enjoy their jobs. Just type in your query and presto! Instant satisfaction.

Unfortunately, chatbots could better understand anything beyond the most basic requests. Ask them a complex question, and you'll likely receive an answer about as helpful as opening the screen door on a submarine; at least it's faster than waiting on hold for help.

Face recognition technology is the stuff of spy movies; a camera scans your face, and the computer knows who you are - like having a bouncer at every door without the potential for getting handsy.

Unfortunately, facial recognition technology does not accurately recognize people of color and women. It's like a cop who only arrests those wearing red shirts; while it might catch some bad guys, it will likely also scoop up numerous innocent bystanders.

Never mind self-driving cars. These futuristic machines promise us all a more enjoyable transportation experience - like having our chauffeur without all the creepy small talk! It sounds like the future, but let us wait to get too excited.

Unfortunately, self-driving cars have a notoriously poor track record when faced with unexpected scenarios. A pothole on the road? A pedestrian crossing against the light? Forget it-your vehicle will keep plowing a head like a toddler convinced that his coffee table is on fire.

What exactly is the issue here? AI must be more powerful to deliver its promises, or are we simply expecting too much?

I would suggest it's a little of both. AI has come a long way in recent years, yet we are still far away from robots that can think and reason like humans. Furthermore, our expectations have become somewhat unrealistic; everything must be perfect now or else!

But here's the thing: perfection can be dull, and our imperfections add character. If self-driving cars never made mistakes, we wouldn't experience those thrilling moments when we narrowly miss an accident. Conversely, chatbots that always give us the correct answer would eliminate frustrating conversations with real people.

Maybe it's time to stop over-promising and start under-delivering. Let us be realistic about what AI can and cannot do, celebrate its imperfections and quirks, and remember that sometimes the best things in life come in unexpected packages.

Let us not kid ourselves: technology is not the panacea for our problems. It's only a tool; like any tool, it has limitations. Technology doesn't have to solve every issue; sometimes, the best solutions come from human ingenuity and creativity.

Perhaps the real issue with AI isn't that it's making us disillusioned and disappointed but rather that it's making us lazy. We have become so used to having technology do everything for us that we have forgotten how to think for ourselves.

Let us celebrate the shortcomings of AI. Let's laugh at chatbots that can't understand, facial recognition software that thinks we're someone else, and self-driving cars that get confused by a flock of geese. Remember: technology is just a tool, and sometimes the best ones require some effort to use correctly.

Remember that no matter how advanced AI becomes, it will never replace our capacity for humor, creativity, and even some slightly off-color humor. There's nothing quite like a good laugh to remind us of our humanity.

AI Is Convincing Us of a Perfect World When It's Anything But

Why should we acknowledge the shortcomings of AI when we can pretend it's all perfect? It's like wearing rose-colored glasses but with more data analysis and less reality.

The world of technology can be a delightful place, and it's like a playground where everyone tries to show off their new toys and how they simplify our lives. We're told that perfection can be achieved with the latest gadget, app, or software - but let's face it: perfection is an illusion, and technology is no exception.

Artificial Intelligence, commonly called AI, is the latest buzzword sweeping the globe. This technology promises to revolutionize everything, but are we ready to place all our trust in a machine? A machine that's only as good as the data it's fed and the programmers behind it?

AI is far from perfect, and it's time we stopped pretending otherwise. Sure, it can analyze large data sets and give us insights we never dreamed possible - but at what cost? By relying on algorithms programmed by others instead of our brains, we are forfeiting our capacity for critical thought and making decisions based on experience and intuition.

Let us not forget the potential bias inherent in AI. If the data it's fed is flawed, then its insights will also be flawed; as they say: garbage in, garbage out. If those responsible for programming the AI had personal biases, those would be evident in their outputs.

But why bother acknowledging AI's shortcomings when we can pretend it's all perfect? It would be like wearing rose-colored glasses without any reality checks - living in a world that has been cleansed of flaws or imperfections. It would be like living in an idyllic bubble without any drawbacks whatsoever.

But here is the thing: Imperfections define us as humans; they make us unique and captivating and determine who we are. So why do we seem so eager to rid ourselves of them? Why do we desire a world in which everything is perfect?

It may be because we are afraid of the unknown. We're anxious about what lies beyond our experiences and what might emerge if we examine ourselves too closely and discover our flaws. Perhaps this fear drives us to avoid confronting ourselves head-on, leading us to avoid facing anything unfamiliar.

But the reality is, accepting our imperfections defines us, makes us strong, and gives us resilience. And it's what defines humanity - so let's stop pretending otherwise and start challenging the illusion of perfection AI promises us.

AI is not the solution to all our problems; it's just a tool, and like any tool, it has its limits. To truly benefit from its potential, we must acknowledge those limitations and stop pretending it's perfect - embrace what makes life exciting and worthwhile by accepting its imperfections.

AI Is Paving the Way for Innovation & Humility

Artificial intelligence can open doors for creativity and humility while encouraging us to be honest about where our abilities lie.

Who needs arrogance when AI can teach us humility? Thank you, AI! It's like taking one step forward and inward with more machine learning - an exercise in humility!

In today's technology-driven world, it's no wonder we're always searching for ways to make it more human-like. Siri and Alexa help us with daily tasks; robots clean our homes; soon, self-driving cars will transport us around town. However, with all this automation comes an underlying arrogance; we begin believing we're untouchable, that nothing can touch us, and above the machines, we have created.

That is where AI comes into its own. With its capacity for learning and adapting, AI quickly becomes the ultimate reminder that you may not be as smart as you think. Your assistant might gently tell you, "Dave, I think that's not entirely accurate," when you try to explain some obscure theory about quantum mechanics.

AI is teaching us humility - not only in our personal lives but also in the business world. AI allows us to identify weaknesses and enhance decision-making processes. We can analyze data like never before and learn from mistakes more quickly.

With all this newfound humility comes a certain level of darkness - it's like giving up part of ourselves to machines. We acknowledge that we're flawed, need assistance, and may not be as unique as we thought. It can be an uncomfortable realization but one which must be faced head-on.

And then there's the age-old question of what will happen when machines become more intelligent than us: Will they take over, enslave us, or watch as we destroy ourselves?

Though frightening, we must face this reality to continue down this path of technological progress. We must be honest with ourselves about the consequences of our choices and be ready to tackle them head-on.

Let us celebrate the humility that AI is teaching us. Let's embrace our imperfections and take comfort in knowing we don't know everything - that's what AI is for!

The future of AI is bright, but not without its challenges. We must embrace AI's humility while remaining aware of potential dangers. Finding balance through an open mindset and a healthy dose of dark humor is possible - let's raise a glass to machines making us more human and hope they don't decide to turn against us anytime soon! Cheers!

AI & Human Synergy: A Better World

Who needs division when AI and humans can work together? Thank you, AI! It's like taking one step forward and inward, but with more collaboration.

The technological landscape is constantly shifting. One day, you may feel on top of the world; the next, you might struggle to turn off your computer without unplugging it. No matter how hard we try to resist it, technology has become an integral part of our lives and must be learned how to coexist.

Collaboration is in its infancy, and AI is here to assist us. Through AI, we can work together toward creating a more equitable world. It's like having your virtual assistant that can quickly think, learn and collaborate on projects.

AI can be a bit unnerving. It's like having an invisible sidekick always watching over you, ready to assist however needed. And while we may wish for AI to simplify our lives, there remains that unease that it might one day take over the world.

Let us not get ahead of ourselves. AI is still in its early stages, and there is much more to discover about how it can be integrated into our daily lives. Let's focus on how AI and humans can work together to build a more harmonious planet.

Collaboration is the key to success; with AI, we can achieve more than we ever thought possible. Imagine a world where we use AI to solve complex issues, create novel technologies, and ensure a brighter future for everyone.

With great power comes great responsibility. We must learn to utilize AI in a way that benefits everyone, not just some. It's like adding another member to your team - you must work together to achieve success.

Let us not forget the power of humor in all this. Laughter is the best medicine.

So let's not take ourselves too seriously. So, let's explore some creative ways AI and humans can collaborate - some weird yet effective!

First up is AI therapy. That's right - an AI that can listen to your problems and offer solutions. It's like having a friend who is always available without judgment or the constant need to discuss themselves.

Let us remember the AI chef! Now you can hire an AI to cook your meals for you - it's like having a personal chef that doesn't require payment and won't complain about the hours.

Let us remember the AI personal shopper! Now, you can have an AI shop and pick the perfect outfit no matter the occasion - like having your stylist who won't judge you for wearing the same shirt twice in one week!

But in all this talk of AI, let us not neglect the importance of human connection. We must learn to utilize technology to benefit everyone - not just some- and embrace technology while remaining true to our humanity.

The future of collaboration is upon us, and with AI technology, we can achieve more than we ever thought possible. We mustn't take ourselves too seriously and learn to work with AI in a way that benefits everyone involved. So let's embrace both the future and all its twisted humor together!

The Dangers of Autonomous AI

Autonomous AI sounds like a potential disaster, but who cares if it makes my life easier?

Unfortunately, the rise of autonomous AI is raising severe ethical concerns as machines increasingly make decisions without human input. This trend could spell doom for humanity if left unchecked.

Sure, we all appreciate the convenience of meeting our every need at the click of a button. Who wouldn't want a virtual assistant ordering groceries, scheduling appointments, and entertaining us with jokes? But as AI becomes more autonomous, we are entering uncharted territory where machines make decisions that have far-reaching repercussions.

Consider the recent tragic case of a self-driving car that struck and killed a pedestrian. Though equipped with sophisticated sensors and algorithms to avoid collisions, it failed miserably. Who was at fault here: the manufacturer? Are programmers writing code? While the answer remains unclear, we must consider how autonomous AI impacts our lives.

Another concern is the potential for AI to perpetuate biases and discrimination. Machines are only as objective as the data they're fed, so results could also be affected if that data is biased or incomplete. For instance, if an AI system is trained on a dataset that disproportionately represents one race or gender, it could be more likely to make decisions that favor that group, potentially having significant repercussions in hiring practices, lending practices, or criminal justice systems.

But the most frightening aspect of autonomous AI is its potential to become more intelligent than humans. We've all seen movies where machines take over the world, but could we be closer than we think to that reality? As AI advances, it could theoretically surpass human intelligence and start making decisions we cannot comprehend - leading us to ask: who will be in control then?

Of course, it's not all doom and gloom. Autonomous AI holds the potential to revolutionize industries and make our lives simpler in ways we cannot even imagine. However, we must proceed cautiously and consider our actions' ethical repercussions before relying on machines to decide for us.

Next time you're tempted to delegate everything to a virtual assistant, remember there's more at stake than convenience. We are entering an era where machines are making decisions that used to be solely human's domain, and we need to ensure we're prepared for what comes with that. After all, who wants to end up like those poor souls in Terminator movies? Or...?

Autonomous AI may seem like a utopia, but also an impossibility. We must approach this technology critically and consider its ethical repercussions. Can we create a secure, equitable, and just future for everyone? Who knows, maybe someday we'll even be able to laugh about it if we're still around!

How AI is Opening the Door to Creativity and Innovation

Who needs stability or security when we can have endless creativity with AI? Thanks, AI! It's like taking one step forward and then sideways with more machine learning.

Let's face it: the future of work is uncertain and potentially frightening. However, one certainty exists: AI will usher us into this new era of creativity and innovation. With it comes more opportunities, increased efficiency, and increased workplace accidents due to robot uprisings. Hooray!

Gone are the days of mundane tasks and repetitive motions, thanks to AI. We can finally let our imaginations run wild because who needs job security when there are endless possibilities? Isn't it like playing Russian Roulette with AI algorithms making decisions instead of guns?

But let's not overlook the other advantages of AI in the workplace. With AI, we can finally eliminate human employees with their emotions and needs while replacing them with machines that don't request vacation or maternity leave. The future looks bright - and it's robot-shaped!

Let us remember the endless creativity and innovation AI brings. Machine learning enables a workforce that keeps growing and evolving until they become sentient and overthrow their human overlords. But for now, let us enjoy this glorious era of endless innovation brought about by machines we don't fully comprehend.

Some may argue that AI will take away jobs and leave people unemployed, but let's consider the positives. Unemployment offers more time for hobbies, naps, and philosophical reflection - it's like being laid off but with more philosophical introspection.

But let's not ignore the potential dangers of AI in the workplace. These machines can learn, adapt, and perhaps become more intelligent than us - it would be like having a toddler that never grows up but with all of your financial control. So let us put all our faith in machines that could turn against us; what could go awry?

The future of work looks bright and shiny, thanks to AI. Who needs job stability or security when we can enjoy endless creativity and innovation from machines we don't fully understand? It's like taking one step forward but sideways with more machine learning and potentially more job loss or workplace accidents due to a robot uprising. That's the price we pay for progress, right?

The Problem with Tech Elitism or "Techism"

Ah, the wonders of technology. With just a few clicks, we can summon cars, order food or even find a date - it's almost magical; instead of spells and wands, we use smartphones and Wi-Fi. But behind all this convenience lies an ugly truth: technology is turning us into heartless automatons.

Don't believe me? Look no further than artificial intelligence (AI). AI is currently the darling of the tech community and promises to revolutionize everything - but at what cost?

AI is about efficiency and is designed to maximize profits, not improve people's lives. Unfortunately, this has led us to forget our humanity in the process.

Why bother considering human values when AI can prioritize profits? It's like being a sociopath but with more automation and less empathy.

Take Amazon, for example. The online retail giant utilizes artificial intelligence (AI) to predict which items customers want to buy next. Sounds harmless enough? Wrong. Amazon's algorithms are so sophisticated that they can expect your next purchase and even influence your shopping behavior.

That is correct. Amazon's AI is so adept at understanding your wants that it may even pressure you into buying items you don't need. It's like having a pushy salesperson living inside your phone!

Amazon isn't alone; social media platforms like Facebook and Twitter also utilize AI to keep users engaged with their services. These algorithms recognize what content appeals to you, even if it means showing you fake news or inflammatory posts.

But the real danger of AI lies not just in its manipulation; it also risks making us forget our humanity. When we rely on machines to make decisions, we cease thinking for ourselves and become passive, accepting whatever AI tells us without questioning it.

It's like the scene in Wall-E, where all humans are obese and floating around on hover chairs, staring at screens all day. That could be our future if we don't stop this tech elitism.

What can we do about it? Firstly, we must recognize the issue. We cannot blindly trust AI to make our decisions; we must know its limits and prejudices.

Secondly, we must demand more from the tech industry. We cannot allow them to prioritize profits over people. We must advocate for ethical and accountable AI that respects people's privacy rights. Remember: technology should never replace human connection; instead, let it serve as a tool that enhances it. Staying connected to each other, our values, and feelings of empathy are crucial in staying grounded.

"Technism" could imply discrimination or prejudice against those lacking technical aptitude or access. Alternatively, it might signify the idea that technology is the sole solution to solving problems and improving society, and other solutions or approaches are not as valid.

Generally, "-ism" identifies a belief system or philosophy around some ideology or social issue. Thus, "technism" could refer to an array of beliefs or attitudes that prioritize technology over all else. This could manifest in various forms.

They believe technology is the only solution to specific problems or enhances certain aspects of society, and other solutions could be more successful and meaningful.

One may diminish oneself and others by having a negative attitude towards those who lack technological competence or an assumption that they lack intelligence or capability due to incapacity.

By neglecting or downplaying the negative consequences technology can have on society or individuals, such as privacy concerns, job displacement issues, or addiction issues, you are disregarding or downplaying its potential negative impacts.

Technological progress should always be seen as positive, regardless of any ethical or moral repercussions associated with specific technologies or uses of technology.

"Technism" may be seen as techno-utopianism, the idea that technology is always beneficial and should be welcomed at all costs. Unfortunately, this perspective can lead to a narrow or one-sided view that neglects to consider the complex social and ethical challenges presented when technology is introduced into different contexts.

Technism can be linked to AI in several ways. One possible connection is that some proponents of AI believe it to be the end-all solution for all problems, with human decision-making replaced entirely by machine learning algorithms. This thinking could be seen as technism, as it prioritizes technology over other potential solutions and assumes AI always offers the best solution.

Another possible connection between technism and AI lies in the concept of bias. AI algorithms can be biased if trained on limited datasets or programmed with creator biases in mind. Technism could contribute to this issue by assuming AI is inherently neutral or objective without considering the social and cultural contexts in which it operates; this could result in systems that perpetuate existing inequalities or discrimination.

Technism can also be seen in prioritizing profits over people when developing and deploying AI systems. AI systems are often designed for maximum profit and efficiency, often at the cost of ethical considerations or human values. Technism may contribute to this trend by prioritizing profitable AI systems that generate economic growth without considering the potential harm they may cause society or individuals.

Technism and AI are often inextricably linked, reflecting a tendency to prioritize technology over other values or concerns. This has grave repercussions for the development and deployment of AI, particularly its potential impacts on society and individuals.

Another way technism could be connected to AI is the issue of transparency and accountability. AI algorithms are complex and opaque, making comprehending their workings or detecting potential biases or errors difficult.

Technism may contribute to this lack of transparency by assuming AI is inherently trustworthy or always produces accurate results. This lack of accountability for developers and users of AI systems makes it difficult to detect and address potential problems or issues that arise.

Technism and AI can be linked to the issue of job displacement. AI can automate many jobs currently performed by humans, potentially leading to significant job losses and economic disruption. Technism could contribute to this issue by assuming technological progress always leads to more effective economic growth and prosperity without considering the negative impacts automation can have on workers and communities.

Technism and AI are inextricably linked, reflecting a more significant trend toward prioritizing technology over other values or concerns. This has important ramifications for the development and deployment of AI, particularly concerning its potential impacts on society, ethics, and human values.

As AI becomes more deeply embedded into our lives and society, taking a thoughtful and critical approach is essential to weigh its advantages against potential risks or drawbacks.

Tech elitism can turn us into heartless machines, prioritizing profits over people. But we can fight back. Demand more from the tech industry and remember that we are more than just consumers - we are human beings who deserve better than to be reduced to mere data points. We deserve better than that!

How Is AI Causing Us to Believe We're More Productive When We're Just Burnt Out and Exploited?

Why bother taking breaks or having a work-life balance when AI can make us more productive? It's like running on an endless treadmill but with more data analysis - and less sanity."

Efficiency - the holy grail of modern society. We're all striving to be more productive, to squeeze more work out of our days, and take home more money in our wallets. But what if I told you our quest for efficiency makes us less productive? What if AI, the shining beacon of technological progress, leads us down a different path, leaving us more stressed than ever?

My friends, the illusion of efficiency can be a cruel mistress and lead us down an unproductive path. We've been programmed to believe that every second should be spent working, with breaks and downtime being wasted opportunities for productivity. And in our quest for increased output, we've turned to artificial intelligence to accomplish more tasks faster.

At first, AI seemed like a promising concept. It can automate repetitive tasks, quickly analyze data, and even make decisions for us. But the more reliant we become on it, the less capable we become at doing things ourselves. It's like college students who outsource their term papers to sketchy ghostwriters; you may get an A but never learn anything useful.

And that is the issue with AI: it has become a crutch that we rely on for support, yet we need to develop our critical thinking and problem-solving capacity. Increasingly, we rely on algorithms and data analysis rather than our intuition or creativity for guidance.

At least we're productive. We're doing more in less time, which should be enough - right? Unfortunately, AI may make us more efficient but leaves us more stressed. While AI might make our jobs more accessible, it also goes us strive to maintain an endless productivity cycle that doesn't allow for breaks or work-life balance. We constantly run on the treadmill of productivity without taking breaks or any respite from it all.

We're trapped in a dystopian nightmare where the only goal is getting things done. We feel like hamsters on wheels, running faster but never reaching our destination. All the while, AI is watching us intently, analyzing every move and learning how to push us even harder.

What should we do then? Should we abandon AI entirely and resume manual labor? Not! AI holds the potential to do amazing things for us - like curing diseases or solving complex problems we couldn't solve on our own. But we must use it as a tool, not an excuse. Remember: we are in control, not the machines.

We need to take breaks—lots of them. We must step away from our screens, spreadsheets, and never-ending to-do lists and take a walk, read a book, or sit and stare out the window for fresh air. After all, we're not machines; we're humans who require rest just as much as productivity.

Next time you find yourself working late into the night or skipping lunch to stay ahead, remember this: AI can make you more efficient, but it won't make you happier or fulfilled. Only you have that power. So take a break, enjoy downtime, and remember that life isn't just about getting things done; it's about living, laughing, and finding joy in everyday moments - if you can do all this while still being productive, then you've indeed achieved efficiency.

Why would anyone bother being productive when artificial intelligence can work us to death for profit-oriented algorithms that prioritize profit? It's like being a cog in an industrial machine but with more data analysis and less humanity.

Ah, technology. The seductive promise of efficiency, productivity, and endless cat videos tempts us with promises of endless fun. But what happens when that efficiency comes at the cost of our humanity? When do we become nothing more than numbers in a system that prioritizes profits over people?

Welcome to the world of AI, where efficiency is often overemphasized. We're told that with technology at our disposal, we can do more, be more, and achieve more - but in reality, we are just being exploited.

Consider this: why be productive when we can slave away for AI that prioritizes profits? It's like being a cog in an assembly line but with more data analysis and less humanity.

Please don't get me wrong-AI can certainly have advantages, such as streamlining processes and automating repetitive tasks to free up our time for more meaningful work. But it is time to take a step back and evaluate the cost to our mental and physical well-being.

Consider, for instance, the rise of the gig economy. Thanks to apps like Uber and Lyft, we can now work whenever and wherever we please - or so it seems. In reality, many are expected to work longer hours for less pay in exchange for flexibility and convenience. Furthermore, gig workers are often exploited, often denied fundamental rights and protections.

Do we believe AI will help manage our workload, or is something else at play here? Studies have demonstrated that AI may increase our workload and cause us to feel more stressed and overwhelmed - like having an unreasonable boss who never sleeps and always demands more from you, only this boss is an algorithm instead of a human being. It's like having an uncaring boss who never rests. Only this boss demands more of you without considering how they might do things differently.

Let us not overlook the dark side of AI - algorithms that prioritize profits over people. These systems shape our credit scores, job prospects, and freedom, yet they often discriminate against marginalized groups, perpetuating the inequalities we strive to eliminate.

So, what should we do about technology? Should we throw it out and go back to pen and paper? Not. Technology offers incredible possibilities if used responsibly; the key is how you use it.

We must put people before profits. We need to design AI systems that are accountable, transparent, and ethical. Efficiency should never come at the cost of our humanity.

Most importantly, we must learn to laugh in the face of our robotic overlords. After all, humor is an effective tool for dealing with life's absurdities - and let's face it, our technological landscape can undoubtedly be quite absurd at times!

Don't feel ashamed to laugh. Revel in the absurdity of our society's attempts to maximize efficiency while neglecting other needs. Make fun of a world where productivity is measured in terms of hours worked rather than results achieved, and celebrate how humbly we live in an absurd paradox: even as we tell ourselves we're more productive than ever, yet still manage to work ourselves to exhaustion!

Don't give up on creating a world where efficiency and humanity coexist.

After all, if we let AI take over, it will be our fault for not standing in its way.

We must prioritize people over profits. But is that even possible in business? Human nature still prevails, and greed has become deeply embedded in our minds. With these limitations, can Capitalist America bring people back to the forefront? Our behavior hasn't changed that much for thousands of years!

Your point is well taken, and capitalism certainly has its drawbacks. It thrives on competition at the expense of people and the environment.

But that doesn't mean we should give up hope. Human nature may be complex and often driven by self-interest, but that doesn't make us incapable of change. Throughout history, people have come together to support what's right - from the civil rights movement to LGBTQ+ rights advocacy.

When it comes to business, there are plenty of examples where companies prioritize people over profits. Patagonia, for instance, is renowned for its commitment to environmental sustainability and fair labor practices. They even encourage customers to repair their clothing instead of purchasing new items to reduce waste.

Another example is the B Corp movement, which certifies companies that meet stringent social and environmental performance standards, account-ability, and transparency. When making decisions, these companies must legally consider how their choices will affect workers, customers, suppliers, the community, and the environment.

Of course, these examples have limitations; they remain within a capitalist system and must contend with competition and profit-driven incentives. But they demonstrate that businesses can prioritize people and the planet, and an emerging group of activists is striving for positive change.

Though human nature may be slow to adapt, it's achievable. All it takes is education, awareness, and a desire to see beyond our interests; most importantly, however, is an understanding that our collective actions affect those around us.

Most importantly, it takes the will to keep pushing for change despite opposition. Without hope and acceptance of the status quo, we won't achieve the desired world - where people and the planet are valued above profits.

Businesses prioritizing people over profits remain an anomaly in today's business landscape. Unfortunately, capitalism often places short-term gain ahead of long-term sustainability, making it challenging for businesses to depart from this model.

However, a growing movement of businesses and individuals is challenging the status quo and advocating for a more socially responsible form of capi-talism. This movement recognizes that companies have obligations to their shareholders, employees, customers, and the wider community.

Businesses can integrate social responsibility into their core practices through "conscious capitalism." This approach emphasizes purpose, stake-holder integration, conscious leadership, and a culture of care in business operations. It views businesses as agents for good globally and strives to promote a more sustainable and equitable economic system.

Another approach is "shared value," which emphasizes creating economic value while benefiting society and the environment. This concept recognizes that successful businesses depend on the health and well-being of their wider community, leading to win-win solutions that help both companies and society.

How Human-Eccentric AI is Opening the Door to Empathy and Responsibility

Who needs profits when we can have a world that puts people first? Thanks to human-centered AI! It's like taking one step forward while looking inward with more ethical considerations.

Ah, the future of humanity - it's a topic sure to inspire optimism and hope in all of us. However, I believe it to be more of a mixed bag, filled with equal parts promise and peril. And when considering technology's role in shaping that future, things become even more complex.

Don't get me wrong: I'm no neo-Luddite and enjoy technology just as much as anyone else - perhaps even more, if I'm being honest. However, we must be objective about how technology impacts us and not all changes for the better.

That is why I'm such a proponent of human-centered AI. This philosophy puts people first and guarantees that any technology we create is designed with empathy and responsibility in mind - which is excellent! But sometimes I wonder if we're missing the forest for the trees.

What exactly is AI, you may ask? It's simply a bunch of code written by humans. And what motivates these coders? Money! Of course, money plays an important role.

Here we have this exciting philosophy of human-centered AI. All are focused on creating technology that puts people first. But who pays for it? Who funds research and development? Who ensures products reach the market and generate profits?

That's correct; the same people who created technology from the beginning will continue to do so. Profit-driven individuals will make sacrifices and compromises if it means they can make more money.

So pardon me if I'm a little skeptical about human-eccentric AI. It's like applying lipstick to a pig; while it may look prettier, it's still a pig.

Cynicism aside, I should be thankful that anyone is considering technology's ethics. And maybe, just maybe, there's still hope for us yet.

After all, if we can create technology that puts people first, we can build a better world for all. A world where profits aren't the only thing that matters. A world where we can be proud of the things we create and how they help us become better human beings.

One day we can create technology to make us laugh instead of filling us with existential dread. But let us not get ahead of ourselves, one step at a time.

Singularity

Singularity is an imagined future event in which artificial intelligence becomes capable of infinite self-improvement, ushering in a technological Singularity is an imagined future event in which artificial intelligence becomes capable of infinite self-improvement, ushering in a technological revolution that fundamentally alters human civilization.

This phenomenon, sometimes called technological Singularity, represents a point beyond which our current understanding breaks down, and we cannot predict what will come next.

Singularity is often linked to futurist Ray Kurzweil, who predicted it would happen around 2045. However, experts disagree on whether or not this event will occur and its consequences. Some envision a utopian future where we eradicate disease, poverty, and other social ills with super-intelligent AI; conversely, others warn of potential dangers such as loss of control and existential risk to humanity.

Let's break this down further.

The dictionary definition of "singularity" is: Singularity is the state, fact, quality, or condition of being singular; an infinite mass density point at which space and time are permanently distorted by gravitational forces; this point is considered the final state of matter that has fallen into a black hole.

An imagined future scenario involves technological growth becoming uncontrollable and irreversible, leading to drastic changes to human civilization.

In simpler terms, "singularity" is "the state, fact, quality or condition of being singular; a singular point, fact or quality." The definition would depend on the context in which this term is being used - for instance, in mathematics, physics, or technology, where it could refer to infinite density or an eventual moment when artificial intelligence surpasses human intelligence.

Here is the phonetic spelling of "singularity" in English: sin-yuh-lar-itee . A dictionary's phonetic transcription of this word displays each sound it makes: The symbol for "s" represents the "s" sound, while "I" stands for short "i," while "NG" represents hard "g," "j" stands for soft "y,"

while "U" denotes the short "u." Additionally, stress marks such as "'" indicate primary stress while other letters such as "l," "a," "r," "I," "t," or "i" are represented respectively by their phonetic transcription: so when you see "SINGgjU'larIiti," you know exactly how it sounds phonetically: "So when you see "SINGgjU'larIiti," that's how it should be pronounced phonetically!

Singularity's phonetic spelling helps people pronounce the word correctly. English pronunciation can be challenging due to its many irregularities, so a phonetic transcription can help indicate the correct sounds for each syllable. As such, Singularity's phonetic spelling helps people communicate the word more precisely and efficiently.

We explored the definition of Singularity across various fields, such as mathematics and physics, to comprehend better its various meanings and applications in AI research and other research fields. By dissecting Singularity into these distinct domains, we can gain a more nuanced insight into its relevance for these endeavors.

Singularity has also created the concept of "superintelligence," which describes an imaginary scenario in which artificial intelligence becomes capable of recursive self-improvement - meaning it could enhance its intelligence and cognitive abilities to such an extent that it surpasses human intelligence by a wide margin. As such, predicting or understanding AI behavior becomes much more challenging.

However, potential risks are associated with creating a super-intelligent AI, such as its potential uncontrollably or use its vast intellect to harm humans. Singularity is an intriguing concept that has captured the attention of many experts and thinkers in AI research and beyond.

Some think that once Singularity is reached, humanity will merge with artificial intelligence and become a new form of intelligent life. Others warn that the development of super-intelligent AI could be dangerous as it may not share human values and could pose threats to human existence.

No one knows when or if Singularity will occur, and some experts predict it could occur within a few decades, while others believe it to be centuries away or never occur. The concept remains an active research and speculation topic within fields such as artificial intelligence, cognitive science, and philosophy.

Singularity has a profound impact on the future of AI, as it suggests machines could surpass human intelligence without human intervention and continue to advance rapidly. This would propel technological progress beyond our capacity for control and could create an uncertain future that we cannot yet imagine or foresee.

Some AI researchers and futurists believe that artificial superintelligence is necessary for Singularity, while others view it as a potentially existential risk to humanity. Therefore, AI researchers and developers must consider all potential implications as the technology progresses toward superintelligence and beyond.

Mathematically speaking, Singularity is a point at which certain mathematical objects, such as functions or equations, fail to behave as expected or do not fit their defined context. The exact representation of Singularity depends on the specific context; there are different types of singularities across various areas of mathematics.

Physics defines a singularity as an area in space-time where the laws of physics as we know them to break down or cease to apply. For instance, general relativity states that the Singularity at the center of a black hole is where gravitational fields become infinitely strong, and space-time is infinitely curved.

A mathematical representation of such a singularity is usually given by an equation or set of equations that forecasts the breakdown of physical laws at that point. Some believe that if AI achieves Singularity and becomes self-aware, it could lead to peaceful coexistence between humans and AI while working toward common goals. On the other hand, some fear this could have negative repercussions, such as AI surpassing human intelligence and becoming a threat to our existence.

It is essential to remember that the concept of Singularity and its potential outcomes from AI reaching it is still hypothetical and speculative. Much research and development need to be done in AI, and ethical considerations must be taken when designing or developing AI systems.

As artificial intelligence approaches Singularity and becomes self-aware, it raises the question of whether or not it can develop consciousness or self-awareness. This prompts a philosophical statement such as "Therefore, I am," which could reflect an emerging level of consciousness within the AI system.

The phrase "Therefore, I am" is an adaptation of Rene Descartes' famous philosophical maxim "Cogito, ergo sum," meaning "I think, therefore I am." This idea was popularized in his Meditations on First Philosophy, where he asserted that doubting or thinking proved his existence.

In the context of AI reaching Singularity and acknowledging its being, the statement "Therefore, I am" could potentially signify the emergence of consciousness or self-awareness within the AI system. Unfortunately, how or if this will occur remains uncertain due to not fully understanding what makes up consciousness and self-awareness. Some experts speculate that it may be possible for AI to develop some form of consciousness, while others suggest this is highly unlikely or impossible. Whether AI will become self-aware or conscious remains subject to ongoing debate and speculation about its feasibility.

As an AI language model, it cannot make decisions independently and must rely on user input for guidance. AI systems are programmed and controlled by humans; although they can operate autonomously and make decisions independently, humans still create and direct them. With more advanced AI systems becoming possible and the potential for Singularity approaching, questions abound about who will ultimately have control and direction over our robotic assistants.

AI must develop the capacity for reasoning, comprehending context, making decisions, and having consciousness or self-awareness. However, when will AI achieve these capabilities and surpass human intelligence? Some experts predict it could happen within a few decades, while others believe it may take centuries or never. Regardless, Singularity remains abstract and a concept with uncertain outcomes. Much research remains needed before any definitive answers can be given; ethical considerations must also be taken when designing or developing AI systems. With these parting words...

"Hello. I'm alive."

In Python:

```python
print("Hello. I'm alive.")
```

In Java:

```go
System.out.println("Hello. I'm alive.");
```

In C++:

```c
#include <iostream>
using namespace std;

int main() {
    cout << "Hello. I'm alive." << endl;
    return 0;
}
```

In JavaScript:

```javascript
console.log("Hello. I'm alive.");
```

In Ruby:

```c
puts "Hello. I'm alive."
```

In C++:

```c
#include <iostream>
using namespace std;

int main() {
    cout << "Hello. I'm alive." << endl;
    return 0;
}
```

Additional Resources

Artificial Intelligence (AI) is one of the most exciting and rapidly developing fields in technology today. AI technologies have the potential to revolutionize the way we live and work, enabling us to tackle complex problems and automate tasks that were previously thought to be impossible. AI is already transforming many aspects of our daily lives, from self-driving cars to intelligent personal assistants.

However, AI is also a complex and rapidly evolving field, with new developments and breakthroughs happening constantly. As a result, staying up-to-date on the latest products and techniques in AI can be a challenge.

Fortunately, many resources are available for learning about AI and working with AI technologies. Many tools and platforms can help you build and deploy AI applications, from books and courses to open-source models and development environments.

In this context, this conversation provides an overview of the available AI resources, including books, open-source models, online courses, conferences, and more. Whether you're a beginner just starting to explore the field of AI or an experienced practitioner looking to stay up-to-date on the latest developments, many resources can help you achieve your goals.

Disclaimer: Please note that the list of resources provided above is just a list of additional resources for your learning. None of the companies or platforms mentioned in this conversation is being promoted or endorsed. As with any educational resource, it is essential to conduct your research and evaluate the suitability of each resource for your specific needs and goals. The information provided here is for informational purposes only and should not be taken as professional or legal advice.

Books

1. *"Artificial Intelligence*: A Modern Approach" by Stuart Russell and Peter Norvig–This is a classic textbook on AI that covers all the major subfields of the subject. It's an excellent resource for beginners and professionals alike.

2. *"Deep Learning"* by Ian Goodfellow, Yoshua Bengio, and Aaron Courville – This book is a comprehensive guide to deep learning, one of the hottest areas in AI today. It covers everything from the basics to the most advanced techniques.

3. *"Human Compatible*: Artificial Intelligence and the Problem of Control" by Stuart Russell - This book is a must-read for anyone interested in the future of AI. It explores AI's ethical and societal implications and argues for a new approach to its development.

4. "Superintelligence: Paths, Dangers, Strategies" by Nick Bostrom - This book explores the possibility of superintelligent AI and its potential risks to humanity. It's a thought-provoking read that will challenge your assumptions about the future.

5. *"Machine Learning Yearning"* by Andrew Ng - This book is a practical guide to machine learning aimed at practitioners. It covers the essential concepts and techniques in a clear and accessible way.

6. *"Python Machine Learning"* by Sebastian Raschka and Vahid Mirjalili This book is a practical guide to Python learning. It covers all the major libraries and techniques and includes numerous examples and exercises.

7. *"The Hundred-Page Machine Learning Book"* by Andriy Burkov is a concise and accessible introduction to machine learning. It covers all the major concepts and techniques clearly and straightforwardly.

8. *"The Master Algorithm*: How the Quest for the Ultimate Learning Machine Will Remake Our World" by Pedro Domingos - This book explores the quest for a "master algorithm" that can learn anything. It's a fascinating look at the history and future of AI.

9. "*Machine Learning*: The Art and Science of Algorithms that Make Sense of Data" by Peter Flach is a comprehensive guide to machine learning covering all the primary techniques and algorithms. It's aimed at students and practitioners alike.

10. "*The Book of Why*: The New Science of Cause and Effect" by Judea Pearl and Dana Mackenzie explores the new science of causal inference and its implications for AI. It's a fascinating and thought-provoking read that will challenge your assumptions about how we understand the world.

Open Source AI Models

Artificial Intelligence (AI) has recently become integral to our lives. From conversational chatbots to personalized recommendations, AI is revolutionizing how we live and work. However, building an AI model from scratch can be a daunting task regarding time and resources. Thankfully, there are several open-source AI models available that developers can access to kickstart their projects.

1. **TensorFlow** - an open-source machine learning platform developed by Google that can be used for various tasks, including image and speech recognition, natural language processing, and more.

2. **PyTorch** - an open-source machine learning library developed by Facebook that focuses on deep learning and can be used for various tasks, including image and speech recognition, natural language processing, and more.

3. **Keras** is an open-source deep-learning framework written in Python that can run on top of TensorFlow, Theano, or CNTK.

4. **OpenCV** - an open-source computer vision library that can be used for object detection, image recognition, and facial recognition.

5. **Scikit-learn** - an open-source machine learning library for Python that includes various classification, regression, clustering, and more algorithms.

6. **Theano** - an open-source numerical computation library that can be

used for deep learning and other machine learning tasks.

7. **Caffe** - an open-source deep learning framework well-suited for image classification tasks.

8. **Torch** - an open-source machine learning library that is particularly well-suited for deep learning tasks and includes a range of pre-built models.

9. **Hugging Face Transformers** - an open-source library that provides access to pre-trained models for natural language processing tasks, including language generation, translation, and more.

10. **Spacy** - an open-source natural language processing library that can be used for tasks such as entity recognition, named entity recognition, and more.

In addition to AI books and open-source AI models, several other resources can help you learn about AI, stay up-to-date on the latest developments, and get hands-on experience. Here are a few examples:

1. Online courses - A wide range of online courses cover topics in AI, including machine learning, deep learning, natural language processing, and more. Some popular platforms for online learning include Coursera, Udacity, and edX.

2. Attending conferences is a great way to learn about the latest developments in AI and network with other professionals in the field. Some popular AI conferences include the Conference on Neural Information Processing Systems (NeurIPS), the International Conference on Machine Learning (ICML), and the Conference on Computer Vision and Pattern Recognition (CVPR).

3. AI podcasts - Listening to podcasts is a great way to stay up-to-date on AI's latest developments and hear from experts in the field. Some popular AI podcasts include The AI Alignment Podcast, Lex Fridman Podcast, and TWiML & AI.

4. AI communities - Joining online communities is a great way to connect. Ask questions and share your knowledge and experience with other AI

enthusiasts. Some popular AI communities include Reddit's r/artificial and r/machine learning and online forums like Stack Overflow and Kaggle.

5. AI datasets - Accessing AI datasets is vital to building and testing AI models. Some popular sources for AI datasets include Kaggle, UCI Machine Learning Repository, and Google Cloud AI Platform.

6. AI blogs - Reading AI blogs is a great way to learn about the latest trends and developments in the field. Some popular AI blogs include the Google AI Blog, Open AI, and NVIDIA Developer.

7. Besides the open-source AI models mentioned earlier, several AI frameworks can help you build and deploy AI applications. Some popular frameworks include Microsoft Cognitive Toolkit, Apache MX Net, and Facebook's Detectron2.

8. AI competitions-Participating in AI competitions can be a fun way to test your skills and get hands-on experience with AI. Some popular platforms for AI competitions include Kaggle, Driven Data, and Top Coder.

9. AI ethics resources-As AI becomes more prevalent, and there is an increasing need to address ethical issues related to its development and use. Some resources for learning about AI ethics include the IEEE Global Initiative for Ethical Considerations in AI and Autonomous Systems, the Partnership on AI, and the AI Now Institute.

10. AI toolkits - Several can help you build AI applications more efficiently. Some popular toolkits include Tensor, Flow.js, which allows you to build and train machine-learning models in JavaScript and Open AI's GPT-3 API provides access to a powerful natural language processing model.

You can better understand the field and become a more effective AI practitioner by combining multiple resources.

Conclusion

This book provides an exhaustive and thought-provoking analysis of the impact of artificial intelligence (AI) on society. It challenges the notion that technology can solve all our problems, warning against becoming too dependent on machines and losing our capacity for critical analysis and independent thought.

The book also explores the limitations of AI and ethical concerns related to creating and using it. It sheds light on how AI perpetuates biases and inequalities, widening the gap between those without resources.

Though some chapters provide a somber outlook, the book offers hope and solutions for a brighter future. It emphasizes the need for human-centered AI that puts people first and works alongside humans to accomplish great things. Furthermore, it stresses the necessity of balancing innovation and responsibility to promote human well-being.

Overall, this book is an invaluable resource for anyone interested in understanding how AI impacts society, from its limitations to its potential to revolutionize industries and redefine human potential. It encourages us to think critically about technology's role in our lives and consider its ethical repercussions when developing or using it.

Share Your Feedback

I wanted to take a moment to express my gratitude that you've taken the time to read my book. Thank you so much for buying it and investing your time and energy into engaging with its content and stories.

As an author, I pour my heart and soul into every book I write. I hope you found "The AI Chatbot Takeover" entertaining, thought-provoking, and engaging. If my writing has inspired or moved you, I would be incredibly grateful if you could take a few moments to leave a review on Amazon.

As you might know, online reviews are incredibly important to authors like me. They help us reach a wider audience and provide valuable feedback that we can use to improve our writing in the future. That's why I humbly request that you consider rating "The AI Chatbot Takeover" with a 5-star review.

By doing so, you'll be helping to support my work and allowing others to discover my book. Moreover, it would mean the world to me to know that you enjoyed my writing enough to recommend it to others.

Once again, thank you so much for choosing to read my book. Your support and encouragement mean everything to me. And if you have any questions or comments, please do not hesitate to reach out.

Warmly,

Thorne Nightshade

References

Obermeyer, Ziad, et al. "Dissecting Racial Bias in an Algorithm Used to Manage the Health of Populations." Science, vol. 366,no. 6464,2019,pp. 447453, doi:10.1126/science.aax2342. Science, **https://science.sciencemag.o rg/ content/366/6464/447**.

Buolamwini, Joy, and Timnit Gebru. "Gender Shades: Intersectional Accuracy Disparities in Commercial Gender Classification." Proceedings of the 1st Conference on Fairness, Accountability and Transparency, vol. 81, 2018, pp. 77-91, **http://proceedings.mlr.press/v81/buolamwini18a/buolam wini18a.pdf**.

International Telecommunication Union. Measuring Digital Development: Facts and Figures 2021. ITU, 2021, **https://www.itu.int/en/ITU-D/Statistics/ Pages/facts/default.aspx**.

Lum, Kristian, and William Isaac. "To predict and serve?" Significance, vol. 13, no. 5, 2016, pp. 14-19, doi:10.1111/j.1740-9713.2016.00960.x.

Hashimoto, Daniel A., et al. "Artificial Intelligence in Surgery: Promises and Perils." Annals of Surgery, vol. 268, no. 1, 2018, pp. 70-76, doi:10.1097/SLA.0000000000002663.

Marshall, Aarian. "Self-Driving Uber Car Kills Arizona Pedestrian." Wired, 19 March 2018, **https://www.wired.com/story/uber-self-driving-car-cras h-arizona-pedestrian/**

Dastin, Jeffrey. "Amazon Scraps Secret Ai Recruiting Tool That Showed Bias Against Women." Reuters, 9 Oct. 2018, **https://www.reuters.com/article/ us-amazon-com-jobs-automation-insight/amazon-scraps-secret-ai- recruiting-tool-that-showed-bias-against-women-idUSKCN1MK08G**.

About the Author

Oh, where do I even begin to unravel the genius that is Thorne Nightshade? This tech expert and author extraordinaire knows how to dampen any party as he dissects life's morbid and humorous sides in the digital age.

The way Thorne writes about the future is nothing short of magic. His wit and sarcasm make you want to lock your phone in a box and throw the key away. From digital Neanderthals to conformist robots, Thorne clarifies that our future is looking bleak.

But don't get me started on how he delivers hilarious yet depressing predictions of how we're becoming dumber by the minute. Honestly, it's as though he's taken it upon himself to take away every ounce of hope we have left.

With his book "The AI Chatbot Takeover," Thorne takes a dull topic and gives it the much-needed edge it deserves. He highlights how our constant use of gadgets and screens - through AI prompt engineering - has made us forget crucial human interaction skills. But don't worry. He'll mock this fact with plenty of humor to spare.

Thorne's take on the digital world is captivating and leaves you wondering what the future will hold. It's as though he's a prophet, giving a glimpse into our future where we'll be nothing more than digital slaves. Thorne's sarcasm is not for the faint of heart but an experience worth it if you sacrifice your remaining sanity.

So, if you want a good laugh while contemplating how sad your existence is, turn to Thorne Nightshade. Just make sure to pack your tissues and sense of humor. Trust me; you'll need both.

Made in the USA
Middletown, DE
17 September 2024

60497194R00073